Doing Well and Doing Good

Human-Centered Digital Transformation Leadership

Digital Transformation: Accelerating Organizational Intelligence

Print ISSN: 2811-0552
Online ISSN: 2811-0560

Series Editor: Jay Liebowitz *(Seton Hall University, USA)*

According to a report released by Veritis in 2021 "the global digital transformation market size is anticipated to reach USD 1009.8 billion by 2025 from USD 469.8 billion in 2020. The demand for digital transformation services is expected to rise at a Compound Annual Growth Rate (CAGR) of around 16.5% over the forecast period from 2021 to 2025. The growing adoption of digital technologies, including Artificial Intelligence (AI), cloud computing, big data, the Internet of Things (IoT), and Machine Learning (ML), is driving the growth of the digital transformation market." To be competitive in today's fast-changing marketplace, organizations need to apply the "alphabet" of digital transformation.

The focus of the book series is unique and will cover the various perspectives on organizational digital transformation, namely business & management, technology, legal and ethics, and social aspects.

Published:

Digital Transformation
Accelerating Organizational Intelligence
– Volume 3
Series Editor: **Jay Liebowitz**

Doing Well and Doing Good

Human-Centered Digital Transformation Leadership

Cheryl Flink, Ph.D.
Humansitas, USA

Liora Gross
Center for Creative Leadership, USA

William Pasmore, Ph.D.
Center for Creative Leadership, USA
Columbia University, USA

World Scientific

NEW JERSEY · LONDON · SINGAPORE · BEIJING · SHANGHAI · HONG KONG · TAIPEI · CHENNAI · TOKYO

Published by

World Scientific Publishing Co. Pte. Ltd.

5 Toh Tuck Link, Singapore 596224

USA office: 27 Warren Street, Suite 401-402, Hackensack, NJ 07601

UK office: 57 Shelton Street, Covent Garden, London WC2H 9HE

Library of Congress Cataloging-in-Publication Data

Names: Flink, Cheryl, author. | Gross, Liora, author. | Pasmore, William A., author.
Title: Doing well and doing good : human-centered digital transformation leadership /
    authors Cheryl Flink, Center for Creative Leadership, USA, Liora Gross, Center for
    Creative Leadership, USA, William Pasmore, Columbia University, USA.
Description: Toh Tuck Link, Singapore ; Hackensack, NJ : World Scientific, [2024] |
    Series: Digital transformation: accelerating organizational intelligence, 2811-0552 ; Vol. 3 |
    Includes bibliographical references and index.
Identifiers: LCCN 2023013994 | ISBN 9789811268410 (hardcover) |
    ISBN 9789811268427 (ebook) | ISBN 9789811268434 (ebook other)
Subjects: LCSH: Transformational leadership. | Technological innovations--Management.
Classification: LCC HD57.7 .F5956 2024 | DDC 658.4/092--dc23/eng/20230516
LC record available at https://lccn.loc.gov/2023013994

British Library Cataloguing-in-Publication Data

A catalogue record for this book is available from the British Library.

Cover designed by Brett Wagner

For any available supplementary material, please visit
https://www.worldscientific.com/worldscibooks/10.1142/13201#t=suppl

Desk Editors: Soundararajan Raghuraman/Thaheera Althaf

Typeset by Stallion Press
Email: enquiries@stallionpress.com

About the Authors

Cheryl Flink has held senior executive roles overseeing the intersection of technology, data, and analytics. She led the Center for Creative Leadership's Research and Analytics practice to create new evidence-based leadership research across multiple research interests, including digital transformation. Cheryl now works with global organizations to establish measurement systems and processes that balance the creation of both economic and social values through digital leadership. She serves as an adjunct faculty member at the University of North Carolina Charlotte teaching corporate strategy and ethical decision-making.

Liora Gross leads the Center for Creative Leadership's Digital Transformation practice, where she has earned a global reputation as a thought leader in the development of leaders for a digital age.

Since 2017, her focus has been on understanding what differentiates digital leadership and developing relevant capabilities in new ways, building expertise through a combination of research and innovative practice. She works with senior teams to prepare leaders for current and future digital disruption and to create digital-ready culture shifts. Her experience covers a combination of corporate, academic, and consulting roles with a focus on practical, impactful approaches to the discipline of leadership development.

Before joining CCL, Liora was a director of Hay Group South Africa and led a Center of Excellence for Change Leadership at Dimension Data, a provider of global IT services. She has performed the role of faculty and program director at Henley and other top African business schools.

William Pasmore is an SVP at the Center for Creative Leadership and professor of practice at Teachers College, Columbia University. As a thought leader in the field of organization development, he has published 30 books and numerous articles, including *Advanced Consulting, Leading Continuous Change, Braided Organizations, Designing Effective Organizations, Creating Strategic Change,* and *Relationships That Enable Enterprise Change.* He was the inaugural co-editor of the annual book series Research in Organizational Change and Development and a past editor of the *Journal of Applied Behavioral Science.*

Before joining CCL and Columbia, he was a senior partner with the New York-based consulting firm Oliver Wyman Delta Consulting and prior to that, a professor in the School of Management at Case Western Reserve University and visiting professor at INSEAD and Stanford. He is an active consultant to organizations assisting CEOs and senior teams with organizational transformation.

Acknowledgments

First, we gratefully acknowledge the many team members, sponsors, and clients involved in creating CCL's Leading Digital Transformation Practice. These wonderful colleagues have created a global ecosystem that has allowed us to experiment and innovate in this emerging field. We especially thank John Ryan, David Altman, and Hamish Madan for their encouragement and investment in this new work. We also thank Diana Arokiam, Neel Arya, Chris Beckert, Akiva Beebe, Marc Dellaert, Sean Germond, Wan Liew, Aasha Maharaj, Akshaye Maharaj, Joseph Press, Jerome Relly, Jerard Scorgie, Renita September, and Clemson Turregano for their work in bringing the practice to life. Finally, we are deeply appreciative to our client partners, Rafat Malik and Roger Minton, for embracing the journey with us.

We also note this book would not be possible without the evidence-based research and thought leadership of current and past CCL colleagues. We have utilized concepts developed by CCL researchers throughout the book and wish to acknowledge particularly the work of Dr. John McGuire and Dr. Chuck Palus for their pioneering work on vertical development. Dr. Cindy McCauley has led CCL's research and development on the importance of team direction, alignment, and commitment, and developed the technical manual for the Digital Readiness assessment discussed in Chapter 5. Dr. Stephen Jeong led the validation research for the Digital

Leadership framework discussed in Chapter 3. Jean Leslie provided a critical review and expertise in shaping the work on team polarities discussed in Chapter 4. We thank Samantha Clarke for her skilled research assistance and Shaun Martin for his publishing expertise and guidance. We are indebted to Jay Liebowitz and Lorraine Marchand for their insightful manuscript reviews.

Finally, we are indebted to the CCL clients and research participants who have challenged our thinking and deepened our understanding of how to lead digital transformation in a human-centered way. We look forward to these continued partnerships as we create our digital future.

Contents

Chapter 1

Why Human-Centered Digital Transformation Leadership Matters

The Call to Action

Humans stand on the brink of a technological revolution that will fundamentally change the way we live, work, and relate to one another. This intersection between humans and technology will blur the lines between our known definitions of physical, digital, and biological space, and the rate of change is breathtaking, evolving at an exponential pace. The impact of this Fifth Industrial Revolution of the digital age will far exceed that of its predecessors precisely because of this continually changing relationship between humans and technology. As humans and technology become inextricably linked, digital transformation leaders have opportunities to shape that digital future to create both financial value *and* human value, balancing doing well and doing good.

These blurred lines between human and machine, the rate at which technology is changing, and the profound potential impacts of technology on human beings have created a gap in our current models of digital transformation leadership. These leadership models heavily weight the ability to create financial value over creating human value as we seek technical advantages and shareholder returns. We contend that Digital Transformation (DT) leaders must lead differently.

We must transform ourselves, how we work with the individuals we are privileged to lead, the organizational capabilities we create, and the impact we have on the world. We must begin tilting the balance in favor of humanity, doing well, *and* doing good. We call this human-centered digital transformation leadership and define it in this way:

> *Human-centered digital transformation leadership balances the creation of organizational financial value with the human impact on all stakeholders who create, use, or are economically, psychologically, physically, ecologically, or legally advantaged or disadvantaged by digital technologies.*

The unprecedented COVID pandemic illustrates how organizations have approached this balance and the choices made in creating both financial value and human value during this global crisis. At the height of the pandemic, health care systems became overwhelmed and faced shortages of ventilators, personal protective equipment, and ICU units. Mobile morgue refrigerator trucks sat outside hospitals. Frontline essential workers feared for their lives, while those designated as unessential remained isolated in their homes and stayed obsessively glued to their laptops and phones.

In response, organizations showed a remarkable ability to transform their business models, responding with unprecedented speed. Rolls-Royce converted manufacturing lines from cars to ventilators. Telehealth exploded as health care providers adopted videoconferencing tools and offered virtual services and new apps to manage patient interactions and records. Rather than visiting a counselor or psychiatrist, people could download over a dozen apps focused on mental health. Children learned from home using videoconferencing tools. Developing countries scaled up the digitization of food supply chains. Grocery stores shifted to automated pickup and delivery services. COVID caused humans to live, work, and interact in an almost entirely virtual world. Remarkable innovations occurred as people shifted to the new realities of the pandemic: a testament to the focus on creating human value through digital transformation.

At the same time, there were costs to this urgent pivot to a virtual world. Organizations pushed for survival, reorganizing, downsizing, and demanding more productivity with fewer resources as digital technologies relentlessly pushed forward. Leaders' emphasis on greater efficiency and productivity provoked a backlash, particularly from a digitally savvy workforce that expected that digital transformation would reflect and respect human concerns and values rather than a singular focus on ensuring superior business capabilities and opportunities (Schrage, Pring, Kiron & Dickerson, 2021). The consequences? Increased mental health issues, worker stress and burnout, job loss and financial stress, videoconferencing fatigue, and worker loneliness (Leslie, 2021).

The rapid innovations that occurred during the global pandemic, coupled with the human toll, epitomize the dilemma faced by organizations as the human world becomes increasingly intertwined with technology. While these technologies and systems advance our human capabilities, they inevitably lead to real dilemmas. In a Pew Research Foundation report, more than 530 innovators and pioneers in technology reflected on this dilemma (Stansberry, Anderson, & Rainie, 2019). Their remarks point to the critical need to create a fair and equitable digital future, and the onus for creating that future depends on each of us. These digital leaders see the enormous potential benefits of technology to enhance human well-being through longer healthy lifespans, greater leisure, and more equitable distributions of wealth. They also see the existential crisis looming from climate change. And they believe that corporations have a duty to engage in creating both financial and human value. We agree.

Balancing Doing Well and Doing Good

In this book, we argue that digital transformation leaders and their organizations must invest in developing human-centered leadership capabilities that span multiple levels of the organization and that by doing so, leaders and organizations will be better equipped to understand and optimize the human impact of technology. This leadership orientation will require engaging an entire system of stakeholders, including those who set the vision, strategy, and digital transformation mandate; develop and deploy new digital technologies; and benefit from or are adversely affected by new digital technologies.

As DT leaders engage with this stakeholder system, they will inevitably be asked to weigh the human impact of technology's potential benefits against its unseen consequences. We will argue that human-centered leaders must consistently weight their decisions toward doing good when harm may occur. Thus, we define the human-impact decision-making process as follows:

> *Human-impact decision-making is a process in which all stakeholders which have been accorded intrinsic value by decision-makers who carefully evaluate options to balance the creation of both economic and social value.*

Throughout this book, we will call attention to the human vulnerabilities and unseen consequences that must be weighed as we balance doing well with doing good. These vulnerabilities and unseen consequences impact all levels of the organization, from individual leaders to formal and informal teams to the organizational culture itself. They also manifest at the societal level and can impede the achievement of environment, society, and governance goals.

To identify and weight the impacts of the benefits and unseen consequences of digital technologies, we propose four questions that will acknowledge these vulnerabilities and create the dialogue to inform human-impact decision-making:

1. *Who will participate in creating the technology?* The human-centered aspects of this question have several dimensions, beginning with

whether the creators of the technology represent a diverse team with equitable opportunities to share in the benefits of the creative process (e.g., patents, stock options, and bonuses) and whether the team includes the stakeholders who will be impacted by the technology ("not about us without us").

2. *Who will benefit from the profits?* This question incorporates thinking through how the ecosystem of stakeholders will benefit, beginning with the employees of the organization itself. The question also encompasses benefits to individuals whose private data become a critical part of the technology and remuneration to the communities for resources we consume.

3. *Who is represented in the data?* The human-centered questions obviously begin with an appropriate representation of the people who use the system or about whom decisions will be made. Another way we might ask this is as follows: Who is absent from our datasets and might subsequently be left out of opportunities to participate in the benefits or be adversely affected?

4. *Do the benefits of the new technology clearly outweigh the potential negative consequences?* In other words, what is the impact? This question should immediately raise an additional question: How do we know? Human-centered digital transformation leaders must think about how to ask and answer this question with a keen eye toward creating purposeful systems of measurement to understand both the financial value and the human value. Frameworks based on an organization's specific purpose or commitment to environment, society, and governance goals can foster the right dialogue regarding how to evaluate and measure impact.

This is a different way of thinking. It is a different way of leading. And it may seem overwhelming. But we believe this shift to a human-centered model of DT leadership *must* occur as humanity faces the existential threat of climate change, the increasing socioeconomic divide, and governance over data and machine decision-making. This model of leadership should span the entire ecosystem of stakeholders, and so we propose a new framework for digital transformation leadership that addresses three levels of leadership: The senior leadership group that leads the development of the transformation mandate; the individuals, interdependent teams, and organization-level leaders tasked with executing and scaling that mandate; and leadership at the societal level where stakeholder ecosystems work together to achieve positive human outcomes.

The Human-Centered Digital Transformation Leadership Framework

How do we lead the creation of a digital future that balances the creation of wealth with its impact on humans? Before we describe a new digital transformation leadership framework, it is important to define "digital transformation." Let's start with what it is *not*. It is not a deliverable. It is not incremental process change or automation. Rather, digital transformation is a *process* that allows an organization to continuously adapt:

> *Digital transformation is an ongoing process of strategic renewal that uses advances in digital technologies to build capabilities that refresh or replace an organization's business model, collaborative approach, and culture.* (Warner & Wager, 2019)

Let's take a closer look. "An ongoing process of strategic renewal" means that the organization must constantly evolve, adapt, pivot, transform, and change. A process of renewal implies that an organization must be agile and resilient. Consider the phrase "advances in digital technologies refresh or replace an organization's business model." This evokes both a deliberate, thoughtful process for seeing those advances and considering their competitive advantages and the *willingness* to adopt potential new business models. Finally, notice the emphasis on "collaborative approach" and "culture." Human stakeholders must work together to evaluate the potential benefits and consequences of these digital technologies, ensuring they meet the goals of the organization's financial ambitions and corporate purpose.

This definition of digital transformation as a process then sets the stage for a new framework for human-centered digital transformation leadership. Figure 1 presents the framework, and we follow with an explanation of how it all works.

First, note that the model includes five levels of leadership: The senior leadership group, individual, team, organization, and societal. Three of these levels are grouped together: individual leaders, teams (both formal and informal), and the organization. We have grouped these levels together because individuals, teams, and the organization itself must transform together in order to execute and scale digital transformation. Also, note that each level has an

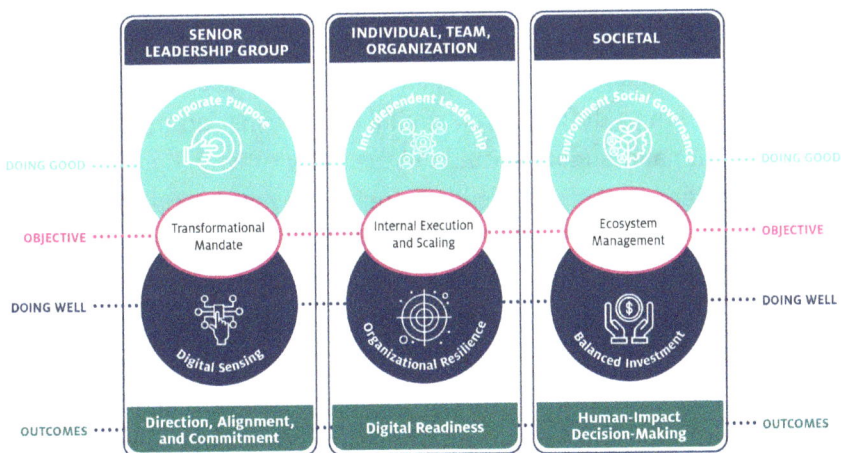

Figure 1:   Human-Centered DT Leadership Framework.

overarching key objective and outcome that must be achieved. Finally, each level of leadership has a core responsibility tied to doing well and doing good, creating both financial value and human value.

Within each chapter, we provide vignettes, scenarios, and short business cases to illustrate some of the core issues leaders will need to address. We highlight human vulnerabilities that will surface and threaten the success of digital transformation initiatives. To address those vulnerabilities and threats, we discuss digital leadership concepts and provide practical advice for addressing them. In the following section, we summarize the core themes of the framework for each of the five levels of leadership and the key human vulnerabilities that will need to be addressed.

The senior leadership group

We have defined the senior leadership group as the CEO, the board, and the executive team. This group, using an inclusive approach, must establish a process for digital sensing that enables the organization to create competitive advantages. Executives cannot be caught flat-footed by a new technology, business model or world event that threatens the organization's existence. This digital sensing process will then inform senior leaders' decisions as they work across the organization to define a new digital transformation mandate. The transformational mandate should tell the story of why digital transformation matters to the organization, including messaging about both financial and human value. When that "why," or purpose, clearly articulates both the story of financial value and human value, the senior team will be united in their direction, alignment, and commitment (DAC). DT may demand restructuring, new funding or acquisitions, different allocation of budgets and capital investments, technical skills development, changes to partnerships, and new sales models. Without DAC in the senior leadership group, digital transformation simply will not happen.

Though we may think otherwise, these experienced leaders will feel vulnerable as they weigh the advantages and risks of digital transformation. Their decisions will impact the future value of the company and can literally make or break their careers. In addition, this group must lead the organization in exploring and protecting the organization from the vulnerabilities of adopting a new business model, such as changes in status and span of control and a potential for employees to lose their cultural identity. As that change occurs, the senior leadership group must be sensitive to both perceived and real losses for both themselves and the individuals and teams they lead. Finally, this group must set the norms for the organization to land on the side of the humans bringing the digital transformation to life. The extraordinary pace of technological advances can create high levels of stress and burnout, challenge existing models for developing talent, and threaten productivity. The senior leadership group must demonstrate that employees are cherished and valuable, not expendable. Investing in the development of digital transformation capabilities of individual leaders begins that process.

The individual DT leader

As the organization begins executing and scaling the transformation mandate, individuals will begin working in new ways. Acceptance that digital transformation is a strategic process of renewal requires that the organization can adapt to constant change. Constant change will present new and very difficult challenges. Individuals need to be prepared to both lead and participate in this change, no matter their level or authority in the organization. In Chapter 3, we present an individual DT leadership capability model consisting of nine capabilities aligned to three process phases: Understanding the landscape, translating the possibilities, and realizing the transformation.

The capability model rests on the foundational leadership concept of psychological safety. Why? Because as the change implications of the transformational mandate become more real, the individuals with responsibility for creating, deploying, and using the technology will encounter many risks, opportunities, and challenges. These individuals will have different perspectives that are critical to hear and consider, but without psychological safety, they will not share those perspectives. Teams must feel safe to share ideas, barriers, and red flags about the challenges of developing and implementing technology; they must also be free to discuss the potential benefits and unintended consequences when those technologies are deployed.

DT leaders can also be challenged by a lack of familiarity with technology and digital savvy. The rate of technological change exacerbates this fear as leaders engage in the complexities of execution and scaling. To address this, we discuss the importance of adopting a growth mindset and engaging in vertical development, an approach to complex problem-solving.

Interdependent team leadership

Implementing and scaling digital transformation almost always requires the interdependent work of team members who span many boundaries, including functions, leadership levels, geographic regions, and skills. These teams may form, disband, and re-form in various configurations because the process of strategic renewal requires fluidity, agility, and organizational resilience. A hierarchical, functional approach to managing digital transformation teams quickly becomes untenable. But no matter the team configuration, DT leaders must help team members achieve four critical goals that enable DT as a process of strategic renewal.

In Chapter 4, we identify these goals as customer centricity, high-performing teams, agile decision-making, and technical leadership. We introduce the concept of polarities, and for each goal, discuss a central tension or polarity that must be balanced in order to achieve the goal. We identify the human vulnerabilities that emerge when the poles become unbalanced: the warning signs that can derail digital transformation. Finally, we call out the current approaches to digital transformation that threaten DT team members and call for a more human-centered approach that addresses chronic stress, burnout, and the fear of technical obsolescence.

The organization

At this point, we will have introduced the building blocks for organizational digital readiness. Individuals and team leaders will have begun working more interdependently as the organization brings to life the transformational mandate for doing well and doing good. At this next level, the organization as a whole must now become psychologically and behaviorally ready to take action. In Chapter 5, we review a model for assessing the organization's digital readiness based on ten capabilities and a four-stage readiness model. We include two brief case studies to provide concrete examples of how organizations have approached executing and scaling a digital transformation mandate. The two organizations are at different stages of digital readiness and have markedly different approaches. However, each organization uses principles of human-centered leadership to balance doing well and doing good.

Societal

Chapter 6 presents the last level in our Human-Centered Digital Transformation framework. We propose that human-centered DT at this level requires managing an entire ecosystem of stakeholders, including private and public partnerships, customers, government entities, investors, and global citizens. We argue that this stakeholder ecosystem must hold itself accountable for balancing investments to achieve both financial goals and benefits to humanity. We have grouped those benefits of human value under the familiar categories of environment, society, and governance.

In this chapter, we also flag the human vulnerabilities that we must guard against at the societal level: the specific "unseen" consequences that can occur when digital technologies are unleashed. We issue a call for digital transformation leaders to convene all stakeholders to discuss potential unseen consequences and to make decisions that at the very least mitigate those consequences, and better yet, provide tangible benefits.

Equity, Diversity, and Inclusion

Discussions of human-centered leadership cannot be had without considering the central importance of equity, diversity, and inclusion (EDI). In Chapter 7, we explore how to change our beliefs and practices to create more equitable, diverse, and inclusive technology teams. We note that today's technology sector continues to be dominated by a relatively exclusive group and argue that human-centered leadership must ensure that technology is invented by, represents, and equitably impacts all humans. We identify activities to reflect on our own beliefs and practices and then offer some practical steps to creating more equitable, diverse, and inclusive technology environments. We also touch on the troubling issue of biased AI algorithms and urge DT leaders to be informed enough about this issue that they can ask good questions, vet potential risks, and mitigate unintended consequences.

The Case Studies

To bring the principles of human-centered leadership to life, Chapters 8 and 9 explore two organizations in the throes of digital transformation. In the first, a startup nonprofit aims to use technology and data to change the foster care system. This fascinating work has resulted in policy change and new funding commitments at the national level. In particular, the case study emphasizes the purposeful focus on creating an equitable, diverse, and inclusive team and ensuring that the people creating the technology and solutions for foster care are the very people impacted by those technologies and solutions: foster youth themselves.

The second case study follows the transformation of a multinational mining company committed to sustainable mining. This organization has invested in developing DT leadership capabilities for midlevel managers at scale with an eye toward changing the culture of the entire organization. We provide examples of how capability development is wedded with digital innovation projects and review the organization's progress toward embracing change in order to create more sustainable mining practices.

Leadership Concepts and Acknowledgments

The Human-Centered DT Leadership Framework includes both leadership principles foundational to all disciplines as well as capabilities specific to digital transformation itself. We note that while foundational principles like psychological safety or DAC are well-known in the field of leadership development, they are not necessarily known by the practitioners leading digital transformation. For example, at a recent technology conference, one of the book's authors, Cheryl Flink, discussed human-centered leadership principles in a fireside chat. When she asked the audience of approximately 100 technology leaders how many had heard of psychological safety, only two participants raised their hands. And yet, developing a team's psychological safety is a critical leadership responsibility in *any* role or function, and this is particularly true as we invent our digital future.

The models and principles of digital transformation leadership have been derived from the authors' collective work as practicing leaders of digital transformation and technology innovation, our experiences designing and delivering digital transformation leadership initiatives to global clients and innovation labs, qualitative one-on-one interviews with senior digital transformation leaders, primary research, and secondary research from academic and business literature. In addition, the invaluable evidence-based research conducted by the Center for Creative Leadership (CCL) over the past 50 years underlies many of the principles discussed in this book. We are very grateful to our colleagues at CCL for the wealth of knowledge they have shared as CCL "advances the understanding, practice, and development of leadership for the benefit of society worldwide."

Conclusion

Every day, we read about the wonders of new digital technologies. Consider the array of neuromorphic computing applications creating intelligent assistive devices like robotic arms for people with spinal cord injuries, chips that can pilot drones based on signals from the brain, and speech synthesizers that translate brain signals into robotic words. Robotics are replacing humans in restaurants, distribution centers, and even as assistants to home-bound elderly citizens. Voice recognition technology now creates facial images of speakers. Quantum computing will provide the power to enable infinitely more complex artificial intelligence with numerous applications. There is seemingly no end to the marvels that humans can create.

These technologies and systems are capable of great good and great harm, and their creation inevitably leads to real dilemmas as organizations strive to create both financial value and human value. Many real-life scenarios illustrate how this tension plays out today: A mining company that must balance its focus on net present value with sustainable mining practices; a law firm that must balance utilization rates and the health and well-being of its employees; a restaurant company that must balance the use of robots to cut expenses in food preparation with worker employment; an insurance company that must balance the efficiency of machine-learning algorithms for measuring policy risk with ensuring fair and equitable outcomes for all applicants; and social media apps that must engage, teach, inform, and protect children from bullying or even suicide.

As organizations engage in digital transformation, leaders have the opportunity to change the way in which they lead. Collectively, we can shape a digital future that benefits humans rather than exploits them. We must, yes, develop technologies that create financial wealth and shareholder return, but we must also diligently guard against exploiting humans in order to do so. And these humans include ourselves, the individuals and teams we are privileged to lead, the organizations we create, and our global society. We hope this call to be human-centered in *how* we lead digital transformation — doing well and doing good — provides a path for achieving a brighter future for humanity.

Let us begin.

Chapter 2

The Senior Leadership Group: Leading Meaningful Digital Transformation

Amanda hadn't signed on to lead a meaningful digital transformation in the global enterprise where she was employed. At the time she joined the company, the word "digital" wasn't even in most people's vocabulary. Yet there she was, heading up a team of people like herself who understood a lot about how to lead a change project but very little about technology. A CDO had been hired a few years prior to lay out the digital strategy for the company, but it soon became clear that she was just one person and that change would require action on the part of thousands of global employees who did not report to the CDO or even understand exactly what the CDO was saying. The new CEO came from a technical background and was strongly supportive of digitization efforts. His vocal support for the CDO's plan did little to move things ahead. Oh yes, people were listening. Each unit leader heard the CDO present the digitization strategy and appointed someone in their unit to get right on it — whatever that meant. Clearly, the CEO was demanding action and it wouldn't do to disappoint him. Besides, moving ahead quickly meant that whoever took this project on would get a lot of positive attention, some budgetary support, and freedom to do whatever they wanted.

After witnessing the disconnected and largely wasted efforts that resulted and hearing from the board about their displeasure with the stalled progress, the CEO chose Amanda to pull together a team that would educate leadership, provide guidance, and support the transformation. Amanda knew that she could not tell these leaders what to do; they were unlikely to listen to her any more than they had listened to the CDO. Instead, Amanda visited leaders and listened. She became curious about what other companies were doing. She curated events that brought leaders together to learn from other leaders and outsiders. She made it clear that she and her team were there to support efforts where there was consensus among leaders on what needed to get done. As her team began to engage the business units, they shared what they were doing and learning. Progress was being made, but it was anything but steady. Amanda felt the CEO's impatience: "Why aren't we moving faster?" Amanda wished she could accelerate real outcomes, but the speed of transformation was not under her control. People had businesses to run and digitization was time-consuming, costly, and disruptive. The bigger the challenge and the greater the potential benefit, the harder it seemed to make progress. Amanda wondered if it would have been better to start over with a separate digital unit than try to change the existing organization. She tried to set goals that leaders would agree to but found it hard to nail down their commitment. They repeatedly flagged too many unknowns and uncontrollables. So she pressed on, feeling at times that she and her team were the only ones putting their careers on the line. When she spoke at external events, people were enthralled by her story and impressed by the progress she was making. Yet Amanda still felt that there must be something more she could do to achieve the CEO's vision for a digital enterprise.

Amanda's experience in leading digital transformation reflects the experience of many organizations. Leaders have a direction in mind but not always a clear picture of what success looks like nor a proven roadmap to get there. While Amanda had made progress, she recognized the difficulties she faced and that success would be nearly impossible to achieve, particularly because no one could define what success meant. Despite a high level of commitment from her CEO, she feared that her job and reputation were on the line. Amanda, like many leaders of meaningful digital transformation, needed help in identifying and pulling the right levers to achieve the CEO's vision. And the first lever to pull belonged to her CEO. Organizational leaders must articulate a transformational mandate that sets the strategy for the organization and results in direction, alignment, and commitment (DAC). In particular, the commitment to digital transformation as an ongoing process of strategic renewal needs to be supported by the senior leadership group: the CEO, the board, and the senior executive team in traditional organizations and the leadership group in organizations like partnerships, networks, associations, or collectives. Without this fundamental support, Amanda will never succeed.

This chapter explores the first component of the Human-Centered DT Leadership Framework, focusing on the challenges and responsibilities of the senior leadership group (typically consisting of the CEO, board, and executive team). It acknowledges the confusion and uncertainty Amanda and many others experience when the objectives for digital transformation are not clear and suggests that the leadership group's key objective is to articulate a clear transformational mandate. This transformational mandate must result in the DAC of the top leadership group itself and then inspire the collective work of the entire organization. Inspiring that collective work will depend on whether the strategic mandate creates a compelling story for how digital transformation will create financial value and aligns with a corporate purpose that creates human value (Figure 1).

If an organization is to undertake meaningful digital transformation, its leadership group must show up as a team to lead the way. This responsibility goes beyond approving a series of episodic projects that produce slightly more efficient systems and processes. Rather, the leadership group must maintain a steady focus on digital transformation despite having to deal with setbacks and crises that

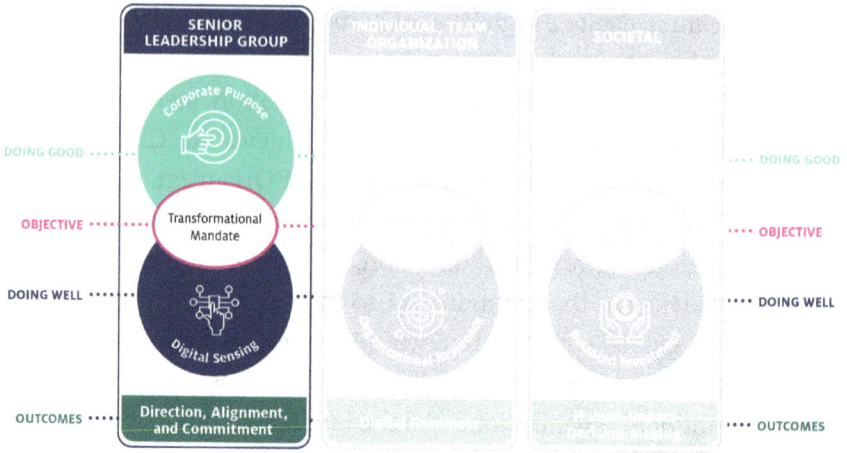

Figure 1:   Human-Centered DT Leadership Framework.

could derail their commitment. Then, they need to find a way to engage others and keep them engaged.

In doing this, leaders must also acknowledge and address the many human vulnerabilities they will feel as they try to achieve DAC within their own team. These vulnerabilities include false agreement, fear of the unknown, and immunity to change. Since penalties can be very high for failed transformation efforts, it is understandable that team members may become nervous at the first signs of trouble and may question their commitment to the process. At the same time, achieving success in digital transformation can be tremendously beneficial for the organization and personally satisfying.

What Meaningful Digital Transformation Requires

Digital technology has the power to reshape an organization's entire strategy for creating financial value and remaining competitively differentiated. However, unleashing that power depends on both the right technology strategy and the right people strategy.

In the opening vignette, the CDO understands technology and has a plan for implementing updates to systems and processes. The CEO is tech-savvy. And yet, the meaningful digital transformation envisioned by the CEO is not happening. Why? Because the senior leadership group itself is not aligned with the purpose of digital transformation in the company. Without a clear transformational mandate, they cannot create DAC among themselves, let alone across the thousands of people they oversee and who are required to make it happen.

In digital transformation, the people factor poses a far more difficult challenge than the technology factor, which is one reason that human-centered leadership is so important. Leading meaningful digital transformation requires a high level of strategic thinking, political savvy, self-awareness and sensitivity to what is happening to stakeholders as the process is unfolding.

Organizations generally have two different goals for the application of digital technologies: (1) to make processes more efficient or effective and (2) to enable new business models to be adopted. For example, the change required for an oil and gas company to upgrade processes to mitigate methane gas emissions differs markedly from making a transition from fossil fuels to green energy. Each goal can entail substantial investment, but the first addresses a component of the current business model while the second creates an entirely different one. Leaders can become confused if they think that digital transformation is aimed at increasing efficiency when in fact it is intended to impart entirely new capabilities.

There are good reasons to invest in digital efforts to increase efficiency. Technologically enhanced processes that depend less on human capital can restore a more level playing field among international competitors when the costs of labor widely vary around the globe. Incremental automation does create added value for an organization but does not set the foundation for a digitally ready organization that can adapt to an entirely new business model.

New (to the organization) or totally innovative (to the world) business models can ensure organizations remain relevant and competitive as the speed of technological change accelerates. Foss and Saebi define a business model as "the design or architecture of the value creation, delivery and capture mechanisms of a firm" (Foss & Saebi, 2017). Examples include Microsoft's shift from software to cloud systems for both consumer and enterprise applications, Disney's transformation from movie production to live streaming, and the University of Southern New Hampshire's move to replace in-classroom learning with online. These shifts are not incremental; they are transformational.

Shifting to new business models raises questions not only about the ways in which business will be conducted in the future but also a more fundamental question: "Why does our organization exist?" Amanda's experience in leading transformational change illustrates many of the challenges leaders encounter when trying to make this shift. Moving from the known to the unknown carries with it a greater level of risk than incremental change. The unknown can induce high levels of anxiety about individual success and career opportunities, create animosity among leaders, and provoke strong internal and external resistance to change.

In most organizations, the decision to proceed with meaningful digital transformation starts with the CEO and senior team and needs to be supported by the board. None of these people have perfect knowledge regarding what is about to happen. At some point, it is likely that the question "Are we sure?" will be raised. If leaders were to answer honestly, they would have to say "no." There can be no absolute certainty. Still, in the name of progress, rational people will be asked to set aside their doubts to support well-informed but untested guesses. Human-centered leaders understand that pressuring people into agreement does not reduce their actual level of fear.

These untested guesses have enormous consequences and are publicly visible. Leaders (including board members, in some cases) *are* being asked to bet the farm. Their reputations *do* hang in the balance. Without a clear transformational mandate that results in authentic DAC, individual team members may waffle as they face the unknown risks of meaningful digital transformation. And yet, the risks of *not* adopting new business models are stagnation and potential obsolescence.

To address these risks, the leadership group must accept three responsibilities (Figure 2):

1. Assess the true need for digital transformation: what we call "digital sensing."
2. Articulate a strategic mandate that identifies how the organization will create both financial value and human value, and why digital transformation is absolutely necessary to achieve both.
3. Create a level of DAC among leaders that will ensure their cooperation in implementing new ways of working.

Meaningful digital transformation involves a transition from the known to the unknown. Potentially, everything about the organization is open to question: why it exists, who it serves, what its products or services are, how the organization is designed, where it operates, who works in it, who its partners are, and even its identity. Almost every organization will eventually face this transition because most business models have a lifespan. The *S*-curve, derived from Joseph Schumpeter's theory of creative destruction (Schumpeter, 1939), suggests that a business model produces increasing returns until it is noticed by competitors, who seek ways to modify the model to their advantage, eventually replacing it.

Often, to the chagrin of established competitors, the disruptors are smaller companies who begin their own quest for success with inferior products but more innovative business models, as described by Clayton Christensen in his book *The Innovator's Dilemma* (Christensen, 2013). Digital innovation has also shortened the

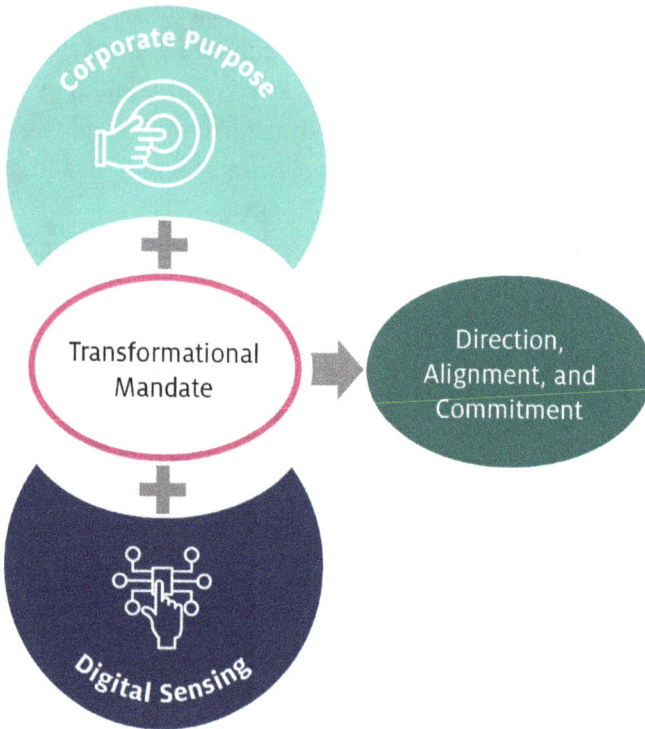

Figure 2:   Senior leader responsibilities.

business model lifespan, creating the need for digital readiness described in Chapter 5. These shortened business model lifespans driven by fast-changing technology highlight the critical negative impact when leaders become complacent. One digital transformation executive noted the following:

We need to be efficient in automating things, and not be losing sight of scanning the market and looking for some bigger, more transformational opportunities. How do we have one of our pillars be externally facing innovation while we're being pulled by the business to just fix things today? — VP of Strategy, Oil and Gas Company

Established companies can be lulled by the success of their business models, then suddenly awaken to the fact that the world has irreversibly changed. Connie Gersick refers to this phenomenon as "punctuated equilibrium," in which everything seems to be going along just fine, until it isn't (Gersick, 1991). When disruption is recognized, companies scramble to respond and do things that may or may not make sense. These might include changing leadership, making poorly vetted acquisitions, offering discounted prices to retain customers, laying off employees to reduce costs, or selling additional stock to generate operating funds. When caught by complacency, many corporations have failed to make the leap forward to new ways of operating, like Kodak, Lucent, Polaroid, Sears, Kmart, Blockbuster, DEC, and Borders to name just a few. How can leaders avoid being caught flat-footed by punctuated equilibrium and/or mitigate its impacts? They can engage in a cycle of continuous learning that we call digital sensing.

Technology is changing so quickly that it is impossible for any single leader to track all incoming competitive threats, changing customer needs, and market shifts; but it is the responsibility of the leadership team to do so. The leadership team can easily get caught up in the day-to-day meetings and tasks required to run the current organization. Instead, leaders must actively be on the lookout for potential disruptions and explore new possibilities *before* they are required to do so. To do this, leaders will need to leverage the board, engage in digital sensing/continuous learning, and create the psychological safety that enables DAC.

Leveraging the board

Board composition matters. The CEO and chairman of the board need to ensure that the board includes digitally savvy members who help challenge and push the organization to identify and vet new business models (Bague, Meany & Lund, 2021). Digitally savvy board members can work with the entire board to ask provocative questions that result in changing the risk conversation from evaluating the project risk of particular initiatives to the business model risk of not doing something new (Weill, Apel, Woerner, & Banner, 2019).

The board needs to question and push the organization on how to best leverage digital transformation and assess the risks for *both* doing well and doing good. Board members can ask questions about the depth of the digital talent bench, how metrics of success are being set, and how the organization is navigating emerging threats and holding to governance standards. They can question the organization's commitment to doing good by discussing the impacts of the current business model on the environment, society, and governance (ESG). "The goal for the board isn't to understand the technology but, rather, to understand its implications" (Huber, Sukharevsky, & Zemmel, 2021).

This open dialogue can only happen when the relationship between board members and leaders is positive and supportive. To maintain that positive relationship, the CEO and senior leaders may spend one-on-one time with board members, load the board with supporters, call on supporters to push their agendas with other board members, use consultants or influential outsiders to buttress their point of view, or create temporary or permanent board committees to assist with specific challenges. Board members are well aware of these tactics, of course, so leaders must ensure that they are transparent and fair in their presentations of the financial and human pros and cons of digital transformation.

The constant evolution of digital capabilities and the expanding range of their potential applications makes it hard for leadership, let alone board members, to keep up. Board members are not comfortable approving strategies they don't fully understand, especially if they are described as "meaningful transformations" or "entirely new business models." The board needs to be brought along on the digital sensing journey in the same way that they would need to be informed of the advantages of making a major acquisition to expand the scope of business activities. And, while most boards do not make the actual decision of whether to undertake digital transformation, they want to be involved. We strongly advise leaders to share their thinking early and often to bring board members along with proposed major changes in the business model. Leaders should avoid the tendency to not engage the board until their arguments are strong enough. By presenting information incrementally and observing the board's reactions, leaders gain a better understanding of the concerns and politics and can adjust the approach. Perhaps the best way to involve the board in the evolving approach is to invite them to join in the process of continuous learning and digital sense-making.

Digital sensing and continuous learning

Learning theorists like Dewey (1929), Piaget (1941), Kolb (1984), and Mezirow (2009) align on the notion that learning takes place in a series of cycles, each involving taking in new information, reflecting upon it, making sense of what is understood, experimenting with it in practice, and extracting new information from action. As learning cycles repeat, knowledge becomes deeper and more embedded in one's approach to dealing with the world. This process applies to organizational learning as well as embedding digital transformation as an ongoing process of strategic renewal: Leaders must always look forward to new business models that create competitive advantage and avoid punctuated equilibrium.

Reading best-in-class digital transformation case studies successfully navigated by organizations, hearing a presentation from the organization's senior leaders, or even immersion experiences can be the first step in one learning cycle. However, hearing about the best practice does not in itself constitute learning. Before the insights gained can be of value, they must be reflected upon (usually through some kind of discussion), made sense of (What do we believe to be true about this now that we didn't know or believe to be true before?), pressure tested in an application that matters, and revised based upon an understanding of what happened as a result, both good and bad. These learning cycles must incorporate both the lens of how digital transformation can create value for the organization and the potential impact on individual employees, the organization's brand reputation, and the entire ecosystem of customers, partners, users, and community. The more complex the situation and the less that is known about it, the more learning cycles will need to take place to produce useful knowledge. This ongoing process becomes one of digital sensing (see Figure 3).

This process of digital sensing must incorporate a balanced discussion of how digital technologies can create financial value *and* the potential benefits and unintended consequences to human beings. Ideally, these discussions will occur within existing frameworks the organization has established to vet and weigh those consequences for individuals, teams, the organization, and society. We recommend that

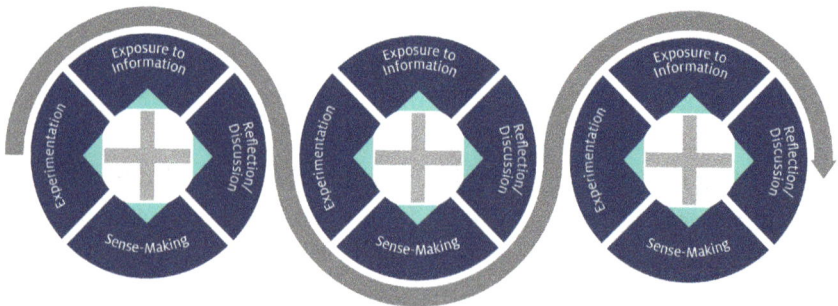

Figure 3:   Digital sensing process.

this digital sensing process includes reflections on the critical questions we introduced in Chapter 1:

- *Who will participate in creating the technology?*
- *Who will benefit from the profits?*
- *Who is represented in the data?*
- *Do the benefits of the new technology clearly outweigh the potential negative consequences?*

Three things about this cycle should be noted: (1) In the face of meaningful uncertainty, one cycle of learning is unlikely to produce sufficient useful knowledge (a.k.a., the right answer); (2) the more rigorous the thought processes and the higher the quality of discussion, the more will be gained from each learning cycle; (3) the faster and more continuous the occurrence of learning cycles, the more rapid the convergence toward useful knowledge.

Now, compare this process of digital sensing to the typical response to forced digital transformation caused by punctuated equilibrium. When an external competitor or unexpected event (such as the global pandemic) exposes flaws in an existing business model, organizations short-circuit reflection and sense-making. Emergency meetings take place, experts provide opinions, senior leaders make decisions based on strategies that are assumed to be correct, execution begins with no specific timeline or process to make sense of what takes place, and no clear measures of success have been established. There is very little reflection and almost no rigorous discussion in the thought process. What follows is typically one big experiment in a single giant learning cycle, from which little useful knowledge is obtained.

Organization X delivered the majority of its services to clients in person prior to the pandemic. For some time, leaders had debated whether to shift to digital delivery as they watched startups and major competitors do so. When faced with a sharp drop in demand due to the pandemic — punctuated equilibrium — the CEO mandated an immediate switch to digital delivery of current programs and consideration of new business models for investment. The senior team quickly evaluated various options for generating immediate and long-term revenue. Although the CEO and senior team seemed to agree on which options to fund and which to set aside, they did not pause to test DAC. Two years later, leaders finally agreed on what the mix of in-person vs. digital business should be going forward. No additional information was used to make the decision than had been available two years prior except proof that the organization could, in fact, deliver services digitally. Some experiments had been conducted with varying levels of success, despite substantial investments. Two years were lost as the team debated the role of digital transformation in the post-pandemic "new normal." The organization survived the punctuated equilibrium of COVID but had not yet articulated a new business model that would future-proof the organization.

Why would leadership teams function this way? By the time an organization accepts that an external event has created the need to shift its business model, it feels like there is no time to learn, only act. Then, the focus becomes *quick* action rather than *thoughtful* action that takes into account all of the impacts. Engagement in continuous learning and digital sense-making can mitigate being caught by surprise. Whether the need for change comes from sense-making or a forcing function like the pandemic, the senior leadership group must have DAC to overcome the significant human vulnerabilities that can derail digital transformation.

The Derailers of Direction, Alignment, and Commitment

The Center for Creative Leadership answers the question "What is good leadership?" by identifying its outcomes: DAC. Direction has to do with clarity and agreement concerning the goals that are being pursued; alignment pertains to the understanding each person or entity has of their role in achieving that direction; and commitment refers to the motivation parties have to do their part in carrying out the aligned actions to achieve the common goals (Drath *et al.*, 2008).

DAC typically occurs in sequence, even though the reality is that all three will need continuous attention. Without clarity on the direction, people don't know what they are supposed to do (alignment). Without being certain that the actions one is taking are the correct ones, it is difficult to engage in them wholeheartedly, especially if they are not aligned with the actions taken by others or have the necessary support from colleagues (commitment). When leadership decides to move forward with digital transformation without sufficient DAC, the risk of failure increases dramatically, as shown in Figure 4.

The size of the circles in Figure 4 is intended to represent the potential for organizational growth. As completely new ideas are tested, there seems to be vast potential for the organization to grow. However, the lack of complete clarity about the costs and benefits of the options being considered can lead to different views of the potential they represent, resulting in a lack of alignment among leaders regarding which alternatives to pursue. If an alternative is selected when the direction is not completely clear and members of leadership disagree with the chosen alternative, cooperation among leaders breaks down and commitment wanes. As it does, the chances for growth dwindle, leaving the organization essentially where it began.

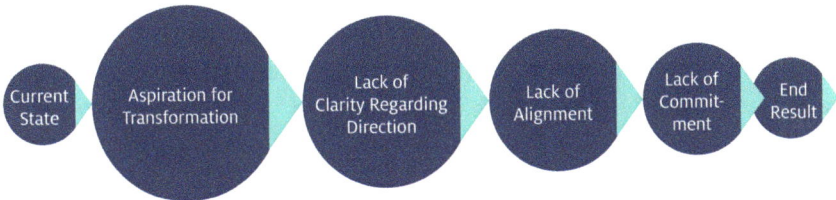

Figure 4:   Consequences of beginning transformation without DAC.

Why might leaders decide to proceed with a transformational digital initiative without sufficient DAC? Certainly, disruptions like the global pandemic may result in pressures for change from customers, the board, or leaders themselves. However, even when new business models have been identified and a strategic path agreed upon, the failure to adopt human-centered leadership approaches can derail the initiative. The very vulnerabilities that we discussed earlier rear up as leaders begin weighing the risks for the organization and themselves. These vulnerabilities can derail creating DAC and stop meaningful transformation in its tracks.

DAC Derailer 1: False Agreement. Leaders may assume that others share their individual views without vetting that assumption. Alternatively, leaders may fear failure but signal false agreement because they don't want to disagree with the CEO or appear to be resisters to progress. This false agreement short-circuits a healthy, rigorous debate that would otherwise lead to DAC and is one of the key reasons that digital transformation fails.

CEOs often lament that their organizations do a poor job in executing strategies, even when they believe that their teams agree on the strategy prior to beginning implementation. However, CEOs may not realize their own enthusiasm can force false agreement. Over time, followers who have not bought in fully may develop reasons (sometimes reasonable, sometimes excuses) that explain why strategies could not be implemented as planned. These followers may pretend to agree with the direction without openly expressing their doubt.

Teams implementing the strategy will inevitably encounter challenges and setbacks that will require regrouping and potentially the unplanned infusion of additional money, time, and resources. ("It's way harder than we thought!") Followers may know about the setbacks but not discuss them openly because they want to maintain the appearance of things moving ahead smoothly and competently.

What's more, leaders may have failed to define what "good" looks like: What are the outcomes that indicate more investment should be made or stopped? Furthermore, do followers actually agree with the goals, or do they secretly believe the goals cannot be achieved?

DAC Derailer 2: Fear of the Unknown. Fear of the unknown is natural. Neuroscientists who study the brain's reaction to threats have helped us to understand that the part of the brain known as the amygdala is activated by the chemical cortisol, inducing a fight-flight response. When we are in the fight–flight mode, higher-level cognitive processes are deactivated to allow us to respond to the immediate threat. We don't think, we run. During meaningful digital transformation, these fears are typically grouped into threats posed by things we do know, like the disruption that transformation will surely bring and the things we don't know. We simply do not know whether we are making the right decisions. Whether we acknowledge these fears or not, they are always present and affect our thought processes.

DAC Derailer 3: Immunity to Change. Kegan and Lahey (2009) have studied what happens when the changes we face threaten not only the future of our businesses but our identity as successful leaders. We tend to push our reactions to threats deep into our subconscious minds because the image we have of ourselves assumes that managing threats is a part of our job.

Therefore, we tell ourselves we shouldn't dwell upon risks and fears. A strong, positive appearance is paramount, and we consistently message "this is the right thing to do." However, our subconscious minds protect us by biasing our judgment to avoid attacks that could upend our self-image, like incoming information that the strategy might be wrong. From our perspective, it *feels* like we are making smart judgments based on the available information. In truth, we are avoiding situations that make us uncomfortable because we aren't in complete control of the situation.

Fear of the unknown and immunity to change clearly operate at the individual level. Fear of the unknown also operates at the group level and can dramatically impact the leadership group's behavior. Although team members may acknowledge the need for meaningful digital transformation and even make a joint public declaration of intentions, they may share fears that they do not acknowledge. Rather than create transparency about the fear and work with one another to address it, they may cover it up or covertly work to kill the initiative so it is no longer a threat. For example, one executive accompanied her team to an immersion experience with leading Silicon Valley corporations to learn about digital transformation best practices. The team returned only to avoid ever talking about the topic as a team again. "What we saw scared the s**t out of us," she said. Rather than address their fear, they ran from it.

Albeit extreme, this example illustrates the impact of our reactions to change that we can't completely control. Unacknowledged fears, particularly on the part of leadership, freeze the organization's ability to move forward. Those fears impact a thousand choices we make along the way without our ever knowing it. Unless the leadership group actively works to acknowledge, verbalize, and confront potential immunity to change, digital transformation will not happen. Since our fears lie largely in our subconscious, we need to adopt mechanisms that surface them so that they can be addressed. Toward that end, be aware of the types of fears that worry senior leaders and their teams.

In research by McKinsey, the authors identified twelve risks and fears associated with leading digital changes that leaders and their teams want to talk about, given the chance. They grouped these risks into four categories (Boehm & Smith, 2021):

- *Lack of sponsorship*: A failure by leaders at the highest levels to authorize the discussion of risks involved in change.
- *Issues with understanding and prioritizing risk*: Underdeveloped processes for identifying, assigning, and prioritizing risks.

- *Difficulty managing change*: Inconsistent change leadership that minimizes risk.
- *Lack of tools or tool standardization*: Nonstandard processes for digital platform adoption and poor attention to the risk of disruption.

Leaders need to carefully listen to others whose jobs and career paths will be impacted by how well a digital transformation initiative achieves its objectives. Surfacing these very human fears is a critical step to creating DAC between the top leaders, the organization's functional leaders, various teams, and the individuals tasked with transformational change. Understanding the fears will then give the senior leadership group the opportunity to limit the "design errors" that the team actually fears. With this understanding of the very human vulnerabilities experienced by the leadership group, let's talk about how to address them by creating psychological safety and creating the "why" behind the initiative.

The "team" — the senior leadership collective — can perform well only when its members experience psychological safety, a concept we will explore fully in the following chapter. Team members must be able to raise red flags, offer their best ideas, take risks while failing forward, and provide the perspectives unique to their functional roles in the company. It is a critical human-centered leadership skill in general and particularly so for senior leaders who will be held accountable for setting the organization's future direction. Psychological safety must be established within every formal and informal team, including the senior leadership group.

If CEOs are to be strong champions for meaningful digital transformation, they must be aware that the harder they push, the more likely it is that their conviction will drive others' concerns underground. Constituents will be reluctant to share anxieties for fear that they will be seen as resisting. At other times, constituents may actually *be* resisting, and the CEO will need to continue to push. Ideally, the CEO will create a psychologically safe place in which leaders can raise concerns so that they can work together on strategies that minimize negative impacts. This proactive work will circumvent the impact that fear — whether conscious or unconscious — can have on progress. A psychologically safe environment is required for senior leadership to honestly vet and address the many risks and human vulnerabilities of digital transformation.

How can the CEO know whether leaders feel psychologically safe?

- First, pay attention to the richness of the team's conversations. Do team members actively challenge ideas, or do they silently listen and leave the table with no discussion? Are new solutions brought forward and vigorously debated? Do all individuals on the team have an opportunity to speak, and if given that opportunity, do they speak? Have there been conversations about potential restructuring concerns, adequate budget, business continuity concerns, existing platforms, and timelines? CEOs must carefully consider the environment that has been created for these open discussions and how their direct reports react to information.
- Second, openly discuss and articulate how the executive team will be supported for risk-taking and potential failure. DT is *risky*. Everyone involved will be making significant bets on any business model that supports a process of ongoing strategic renewal through digital transformation. The CEO and other leaders are literally betting on their careers and the future of the company. Identifying the risks to financial success, brand reputation, employee engagement and well-being, and doing good in the world all must be discussed.
- Consider the derailers of DAC for the leadership group. They include false agreement, fear of the unknown, and immunity to change. A psychologically safe environment can mitigate the impact these derailers have. Psychological safety is so important to leading digital transformation initiatives that it is the central component of the individual leadership model discussed in Chapter 3, where we further explore methods for developing psychologically

safe teams. If leaders have worked together to identify new business models through digital sensing, clearly discussed the risks, and agreed to participate in leading change, then they can articulate the strategic mandate that sets the direction for the entire organization and galvanizes action.

The Transformation Mandate: Setting the Direction for Doing Well and Doing Good

In both our readings of the academic literature about digital transformation leadership and in our conversations with practitioners, we found that DT initiatives frequently fail because there is no compelling "why." Research by McKinsey examined the factors that impacted successful digital initiatives, defining a "successful digital transformation" using 21 different factors (de la Boutetiere, Montagner, & Reich, 2018). The authors found that the largest distinguishing factor between a successful and unsuccessful initiative (by a factor of three) was "management established a clear change story for digital transformation." However, DT leaders often miss the importance of creating this clear and compelling story. One digital transformation leader executive stated the following:

> *The senior leadership team is managing themselves and being able to push down into the organization. So everyone has an opportunity to invest themselves and be a part of this strategic initiative. But ... I've made the mistake myself of not clearly defining with my CEO what does success look like? How will I know that we have reached the goal? If it is not clearly defined ... when you're working on things that are very unknown, you're taking a big risk.* — EVP Marketing, Telecom Company

This perspective surprised us. Without clarity on direction and a clear transformational mandate, why would CEOs set sail on transformative change? We believe it is because CEOs, in managing uncertainty, have a fuzzy idea of what that story actually is, resulting in two challenges to clear communication:

- *The story is not compelling:* DT leaders may struggle with communicating the value and benefits of a DT initiative. Why does it matter? Telling that story impacts the ability to gain team trust and momentum, resources, and visibility. DT leaders need to bring everyone along on the journey (Windt, Borgman, & Amrit, 2019).
- *There is no integrity between the story and reality:* Things fall apart when talk does not match with actions. Imagine an organization investing in a DT initiative that transforms its global supply system for coffee, promising to reduce costs and its carbon footprint while supporting climate change initiatives. If a critical vendor is clearcutting the rainforest to grow coffee, there is no integrity between the story and the reality. Stakeholders will quickly become disillusioned, and the brand will suffer.

The senior leadership group, working with input across a stakeholder community, must tell a clear and important story of WHY: How will digital transformation create *value for the organization* (doing well) and *value for society* (doing good)? The story behind the strategic mandate must have the following:

Be meaningful: Talking about how digital transformation can create monetary value and competitive differentiation may not inspire employees. Make sure that the strategic mandates tie to the organization's greater purpose (van Tuin, Schaufeli, Van den Broeck, van Rhenen, 2020).

Be credible: Credibility includes a clear commitment of resources to both creating financial value and human value and then following through on that commitment. Those commitments may take many forms, from capital investments to policy changes to time allocation to changes in management. Actions speak louder than words.

Be measurable: Metrics like financial profitability, market cap, and net present value are well established and can be part of the financial value component of the transformation mandate. Metrics for measuring human value are emerging as ESG standards become more clear. The UN Sustainable Development Goals also provide excellent frameworks for measuring human value.

The senior leadership group must bring the strategic mandate for digital transformation to life with a compelling story. The presence or absence of that story is central to scaling an organization toward digital readiness, as we discuss in Chapter 5. It sets the direction for the organization and becomes the impetus for the actions that must be taken, from restructuring to investments to mergers and acquisitions.

Reevaluating the Situation

Let's go back to the example at the beginning of the chapter. What could Amanda have done differently to achieve the CEO's vision for digital transformation? First, Amanda could request that the leaders clarify the transformational mandate and how it will create financial and human value. If that clarity doesn't exist, she should insist on that clarity or bow out. If the strategic mandate is clear, she could ask for the details related to alignment and the ability to actually start bringing the strategic mandate to life. If the mandate is not backed by budget, resources, and clear metrics for success, then Amanda has no authority to move the digital transformation initiative forward. Finally, Amanda could have conversations with individual leaders to understand their perceived risks and levels of commitment, then decide whether she has the proper support needed to actually take on the role. Without these elements, success is impossible. Leaders must own responsibility for setting the digital transformation foundation. Without that foundation, the organization will continue with business as usual as time slips away and competitors define the digital future.

Key Takeaways and Actions

(1) Engage in digital sensing to avoid periodic disruption to the business model:

- Shift from thinking about digital transformation as a project to an ongoing process of strategic renewal that uses advances in digital technologies to build capabilities that refresh or replace an organization's business model, collaborative approach, and culture.
- Ensure that your board has digitally savvy members that can help the organization make this shift by changing the risk conversation from evaluating the project risks for digital transformation to evaluating the business model risk of *not* doing something new. The board needs to *push* the organization toward a view of digital transformation as a process, not a project.
- Create and actively engage in a process for digital sensing: understanding new technologies, the potential competitive advantages they may offer as well as the potential risks, and encourage active dialogue and debate. This inclusive process repeats over and over again as the organization becomes exposed to new information, reflects and discusses, determines what is or is not applicable to the business, and experiments. The learning cycles must be rigorous, hallmarked by high-quality discussions, and take place frequently.
- Deliberately create an inclusive model for the continuous digital sensing cycle. This cycle should include a wide ecosystem of stakeholders drawn from employees, customers, investors, partners, and users. To be human-centered, the digital sensing cycles must examine both the financial potential and competitive advantages as well as the potential human benefits and negative consequences. Include representatives of the communities that may be impacted by new digital technologies and strategies.
- When experimenting, ensure that prototyping and feedback cycles actively include not only whether the technology works but also whether it adequately addresses potential harms raised by the stakeholder ecosystem.

(2) Create psychological safety and be aware of the critical vulnerabilities that can derail DAC:

- Encourage and practice psychological safety. Candid conversations cannot happen without it, and no matter how seasoned or prestigious members of the senior leadership team might be, each of them is a vulnerable human being. Measure psychological safety periodically and have active, compassionate conversations with colleagues to identify how to improve it.
- Be aware that without psychological safety within this senior leadership group, three human vulnerabilities will impact the ability to create DAC among this team: False agreement, fear of the unknown, and immunity to change. The organization's financial viability, individual careers, and the brand's reputation and future are all in play at this level.

(3) Articulate a clear, credible, and compelling transformational mandate that creates DAC:

- This mandate must tell the story of why digital transformation matters for both creating financial value and human value, connecting to the organization's purpose.
- The senior leadership team must stand behind this transformational mandate. At this point, this group, using an inclusive process that fosters healthy discussion, must have listened to and addressed the many risks and concerns that surfaced through healthy dialogue. There must be direction (we know where we are going), alignment (we know how we will get there), and commitment (we will make it happen).

Conclusion: The Human-Centered Approach for the Senior Leadership Group

Implementing digital transformation as an ongoing process of strategic business renewal requires meaningful change, not incremental change. In this chapter, we have challenged organizations to protect themselves from punctuated disequilibrium by creating a continuous cycle of digital sensing that is rigorous, has robust discussion, and is fast: all good practices for any organization. In taking a human-centered approach, we recommend that digital transformation leaders do four things: (1) Make digital sensing an inclusive process that brings a stakeholder ecosystem to the table to discuss not only the financial and competitive rewards of digital transformation but also the potential human benefits and unintended negative impacts. This inclusive process must inform decisions made by the senior leadership group. (2) Remember that the senior leadership group consists of vulnerable human beings who will be held directly responsible for the organization's financial and brand well-being. These senior leaders must develop an environment of psychological safety both within their group and across the entire organization to make good decisions that live up to the values of doing well and doing good. No one can hold back their perspectives and views. (3) Develop a transformational mandate that tells the story of how the organization will do well and do good. (4) Ensure the senior leadership group themselves have the DAC to lead the organization forward. Without it, digital transformation simply will not happen.

In the following chapter, we turn our attention to the development of individual digital transformation leaders. We further explore the critical importance of psychological safety and add two foundational elements: continuous learning and vertical development. We include a new capability model that challenges digital transformation leaders to develop themselves so that they can fully participate in and lead DT as a process of strategic renewal, not a project, and simultaneously incorporate human-centered practices.

Chapter 3

Individual Leaders: Leadership Foundations and Digital Transformation Capabilities

The chief commercial officer (CCO) hung up the phone. She was tasked with managing a $40 million client portfolio in the Americas, the revenue lifeblood of the company. The customer she'd just spoken with expressed his absolute dissatisfaction with the new cloud platform, a system intended to transform how the company integrated and analyzed data — and threatened to rescind a multi-million dollar contract. The CCO was ready to resign. In fact, it was the third conversation she'd had in as many days with clients wanting to move back to the old platform. She'd already spoken with the new CTO, who had been elevated to his role after the acquisition of his European company. The acquired company's clients tended to be smaller and less complex than those in the Americas, and the CCO had voiced her concerns that the new system did not scale to accommodate the Americas' clients. The CTO assured her it would — but surely the proof was in the clients' pudding? After several conversations, the CCO decided to escalate the matter and called her boss, the CEO, to voice her concerns, knowing full well that he'd made an enormous bet on the new system. The conversation, filled with denials and accusations, did not go well. Despite the CCO's concerns, the implementation of the new platform proceeded apace. The company *subsequently lost three of its largest clients, and multiple changes were made to the executive leadership team.*

These three intelligent, well-intentioned, and experienced leaders blew it. What happened? The vignette poignantly describes what happens when DT leaders lack the human-centered leadership skills for successful transformation, beginning first with creating the psychological safety required to voice concerns and work together to address them. Second, these senior leaders failed to engage in the digital sensing described in Chapter 2: A competitive platform had created an existential threat and the entire company was now in rapid response mode. They had failed to avoid punctuated equilibrium. Third, the CCO and CEO did not accompany the CTO in speaking with large and small customers from around the globe to understand the actual requirements needed. And finally, the three executives could have had much more honest conversations about the investments required for true scaling, metrics for success, and how to support the client services team members who felt very vulnerable during the transformation.

This real-life example may sound all too familiar. The technology and cloud-based platform were not really the issue; it was the lack of human-centered leadership that led to a highly visible, very costly failure. In this chapter, we present practices and capabilities that human-centered leaders can adopt to avoid similar situations. The practices include continuous learning, vertical development, and psychological safety. These practices underpin nine capabilities that, when scaled across many leaders in an organization, enable digital readiness.

What Is Digital Leadership?

The meaning of "digital leadership" continuously evolves just as the meaning of digital transformation evolves. In the past, descriptions of digital leadership have primarily focused on the technological and operational aspects of digitization: innovation, business models, technology stacks, processes, and customers. This operational meaning of digital leadership is very familiar and one many digital leaders exemplify as they leverage the technical and business skills they have built through education and experience. A second meaning of "digital leadership" is human-centered. This meaning acknowledges the skills required to understand how individuals, teams, and organizational culture can be impacted by the constant stressors of an ever-evolving digital landscape. Specifically, digital leaders must acquire the complex problem-solving skills required to create both financial value and human value. According to the CEO of a multibillion-dollar global organization:

> *We need leaders who will start from a blank page and will build the future without knowing the outcome. Leaders who will create a better world, using technology to improve lives rather than destroy future opportunities for people and the planet. Leaders who will learn and adapt as they innovate with solutions, creating pathways toward the future. Leaders who will solve problems collectively, as today's issues are too complex to address individually.*

After the senior leadership group establishes both the transformational mandate and the direction, alignment, and commitment to achieve that mandate, individual leaders at all levels of the organization must begin the process of bringing that vision to life. Individual contributors, first-level managers, divisional leaders, and the executive team hold the responsibility for contributing to the organizational agility and interdependent leadership required to scale their organization for continuous strategic renewal (see Figure 1). Unfortunately, individuals are rarely prepared to manage the complexities they will encounter as they implement new digital transformation business models. As with the senior leadership group, these leaders will encounter resistance as team members understand the work, the impact on their personal careers, and their own assessments of the

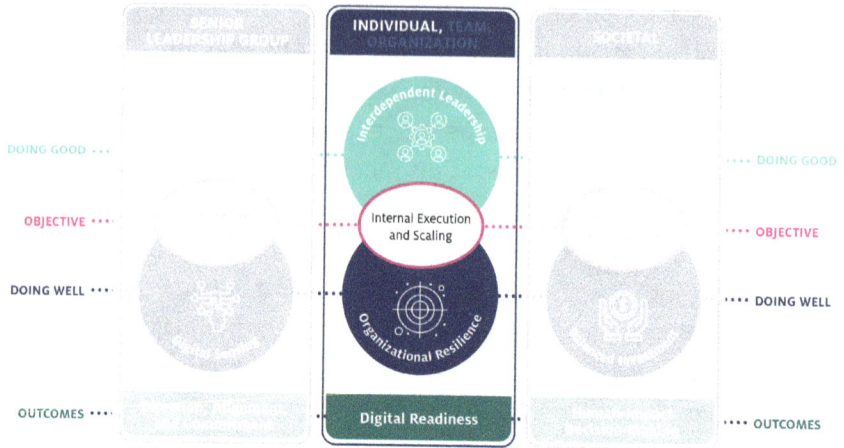

Figure 1:   Internal execution and scaling: Developing digital leaders.

costs and benefits of the new model. With this in mind, we explore a new individual digital leadership capability model, the first component of the DT Human-Centered Leadership Framework focused on internal scaling (Figure 1).

Digital Leadership Capability Model

The Center for Creative Leadership has worked with digital leaders around the globe to develop a new model of digital leadership. This emerging model has identified nine leadership capabilities that fall into three major categories: (1) understanding opportunities in the digital landscape through digital sensing, (2) translating the possibilities into business scenarios that create value, and (3) realizing transformation through implementation. Note that none of the capabilities in this model focuses on technical skills. Rather, the model focuses on the human leadership capabilities so critical to managing in a continuously changing environment. And, at the very center of this model lies the foundational component of psychological safety.

Before we explore the human-centered leadership capability model, we discuss three practices for good leadership that lay the groundwork for digital leadership capabilities: (a) investing in continuous learning, (b) focusing on the individual vertical development that fosters complex thinking, and (c) creating psychological safety for every individual and team. We'll explore these three elements first and then review the specific capabilities of the model itself.

Continuous Learning As a Leadership Responsibility

We expect more from leaders than we do from individual contributors, and the more senior the leader, the more that is true. We expect leaders to know what to do (most of the time) and when they don't, we expect them to figure it out. We expect them to provide us with guidance, make good choices for us, and support us as we do our best to follow them. We expect them to lead change when it's needed, protect us from threats we can't see, and ensure the safety and continuity of our existence. We hope that they will care about us: about our feelings, about our opinions, and about our aspirations. Of course, we are sometimes disappointed in our leaders, but we don't lose hope that they will improve or that the next leader will be better.

Now consider leaders of digital transformation. So many of the expectations we have of these leaders — no matter their level in the organization — cannot be met at the outset. There simply isn't enough known to provide the certainty and protection that followers so desperately desire. Nevertheless, leaders need to count on others to follow them. What separates successful leaders of digital transformation from less successful ones is their response to the challenge of uncertainty. The less successful ones push ahead, projecting an image of calm omnipotence that they hope will instill confidence in the plan. When mistakes or setbacks occur, they downplay them, find others to blame, or just keep pushing forward no matter the cost. The more successful ones do something different; they learn.

Adult learning begins with an openness to taking in new information, something that Milton Rokeach (1960) described as an "open vs. closed mindset." We begin life with an open mindset, but as we grow, we become more certain about our beliefs, whether or not those beliefs are true. Something similar happens as we learn about digitization; we take in information and stories and begin to formulate a view of what digitization is or isn't, how it should be accomplished, and whom it might impact. As that view becomes more certain, we may gain confidence in our decisions but we can also impose false certainty on a blank canvas. As we make decisions, we pay more attention to outcomes that we expect than outcomes we don't expect, leading us to conclude that our underlying assumptions are correct and we only need more time or effort to fully prove them. Our minds become closed without us knowing it.

To keep our minds open to new information that could change our views, we need to adopt a growth mindset, as described by Carol Dweck in her book *Mindset: Changing the Way You Think to Fulfil Your Potential* (2017). We stop being concerned about how we look to others or whether we will fail and instead become curious. We shift from seeing our ability to understand digitization as fixed or limited. We work to improve our understanding of technology innovation *and* implementation, about unintended consequences for the people we are privileged to lead and the users and communities impacted by what we create. We do not force ourselves to appear certain when we are not. Rather, we share our uncertainty with others so they can join us in exploring possible answers. Perhaps most importantly, we don't try to hide our mistakes from others; we celebrate them as discoveries that move us closer to the truth we need to comprehend. We derive energy from the learning we have gained rather than the progress we have made against an arbitrary milestone. We maintain a positive, can-do attitude because we know that as long as we continue to learn from our experiences, there is hope.

Many DT leaders lack the motivation to adopt a growth mindset, especially for learning about digital transformation and technology. When DT leaders don't engage in learning, it can raise questions about the leaders' credibility and motivation. A study by MIT Sloan found that while 88% of employees believed that having a critical mass of digitally savvy leaders was important to win in the future, few believe that organizations are investing in becoming more digitally savvy and that is particularly true for senior leaders (Schrage *et al.*, 2021). The article concludes that "The overwhelming majority of survey respondents assert that their leaders are not prioritizing digital self-improvement." This alarming gap perception will trickle down into questions about leaders' credibility. If senior leaders do not invest in becoming more digitally savvy, how can they ask good questions about the impact of the technology across the organization? How can they vet the impact on the humans using the technology? With so much at stake, why does this digital leadership gap exist?

Experts in adult development like Robert Kegan (1982) and William Torbert (1972) help us understand that the biggest barriers to the realization of our potential as leaders are internal rather than external. Over 80% of us are so caught up in being perceived as experts by others or in achieving goals that others set for us that we never develop to the point where we take our guidance from within. Less than 20% of us are capable of truly independent strategic thinking, and only 2% of us reach the pinnacle of development where our lives are defined not by what we do but by the legacy we leave: the transformations we have led or the impact on society at large.

Simply keeping up with technology further complicates this focus on strategic thinking and complex problem-solving. Leaders can feel vulnerable as they make investments and lead implementations when they do not fully understand the technology. A senior digital transformation executive spoke with us about her work in the field of marketing automation. She works with chief marketing officers leading digital transformation and noted the following: *A number of them told us that they were retiring because this technology stuff was just too intimidating. They just didn't want to learn the new stuff. There's this lack of knowledge and fear around technology and being accountable for technology that they don't understand from a leadership perspective. Imagine sitting at the table with the finance guy and he asks, "Why have you spent half a million dollars on this system? What does it do for us, and how does it work?" And not being able to answer that?*

Digital transformation is not just a matter of setting goals up and knocking them down. Instead, it presents challenging opportunities to learn about what works and what doesn't and to keep repeating cycles of learning to move further along the journey. Learning must be near the top of the agenda for all DT leaders in organizations undergoing digital transformation. Of course, DT leaders need to invest in learning about the new technologies their teams and organization are exploring and developing. They must also understand the structures and processes that currently exist so they can guide and advise as the organization takes on the complex work of integration. Digital leaders need to engage in complex thinking and foster interdependent work across their organization. Formal and informal teams must work together to achieve the financial and human value goals of the strategic mandate. How can DT leaders improve their complex problem-solving skills and encourage interdependent work? We turn to vertical development.

Vertical Development and Interdependent Leadership

The level of complex thinking must match the level of complexity required for the strategic change — and we call that vertical development.
(McGuire & Palus, 2019)

The constant rate of technological change, the uncertainties of an unpredictable future, and the enormity of the potential impact on human beings require that we shift our leadership from reliance on individual, independent leadership styles to interdependent, collective thinking and action. As a DT leader, you may belong to several collectives: the senior leadership group, the leader of the technology team, the executive sponsor of the data governance team, the ethics and compliance group, or the leader tasked with implementing a new DT strategy. No matter which collective you belong to, you will need to move from thinking and acting independently to thinking and acting interdependently. Vertical development provides one path toward that complex thinking and interdependent work.

Vertical development is "the science of how the perspectives of individuals and groups can evolve to become progressively more elevated, complex, and integrated" (McGuire & Palus, 2019). It recognizes that a different developmental approach is required to help leaders thrive in constantly evolving working environments, exactly the kind represented by organizations that are implementing digital transformation as an ongoing process of strategic renewal. When leaders engage in vertical development, they become more sophisticated in their approaches to complex problem-solving. For example, leaders might ask the question "Instead of making this 10% better, how could we make it ten times better?" Or "How might we create new skills for workers who will be replaced by automation?" The required shift in mindset should not be underestimated nor the level of effort it requires. That shift means challenging fundamental beliefs about the way things are and considering very different alternatives to what is possible. It means purposefully collecting different perspectives. And it requires leaders to immerse themselves in new learning experiences that stretch them in sometimes uncomfortable ways.

Let's look at an example. Suppose that a bank has determined it wants to produce a new customer app that automates the process of setting up and managing private accounts. The original specifications for the app require that the team create an AI algorithm that automates the risk assessment for customers wanting to establish these accounts. The technology team has invested in creating a beta product, but deployment has been very slow. Why so slow? To find out, the DT leader shouldn't be focused on asking about resources and timelines. Instead, she will need to dig into the assumptions of those involved to understand the delays. She might unearth critical beliefs that impede progress: "We don't believe this organization has the capability to create and implement an AI algorithm of this nature. It's going to create a nightmare for our brand" or "Customers don't want this type of digital process; they only want to set up accounts in person." These beliefs might be held by the leader, by peers, or by individuals on cross-functional teams. DT leaders must both expose those hidden beliefs and resolve them. Assumptions must be tested, results fairly considered, and when surprising results occur, the individuals, teams, and organization as a whole must be willing to give up their false hidden beliefs and pivot.

Think back to the opening scenario of this chapter: The CEO, CCO, and CTO could have agreed to challenge the beliefs and actions that resulted in a technology system that could not scale: "Large companies do not have more complex requirements, and they will adapt to a simplified system that configures without customizing," or "We vetted the company's technology when we bought it, and it is more than sufficient to give us a competitive leg up," or "Our largest clients will not be willing to give up this functionality." Without exposing these hidden beliefs by naming assumptions and testing related hypotheses, leaders will not be able to move the organization forward. It will be stuck, unable to break through the operating principles of the past that led to stagnation.

So how can individual leaders get unstuck? Below, we describe three practices that can catalyze vertical development:

1. *Heat experiences*: Heat experiences are new assignments, events, or situations where leaders cannot respond using their current way of thinking. These experiences challenge leaders to test their current assumptions and adapt in new ways. A DT heat experience might entail working in a new team that has high-stakes visibility and using tools, such as design thinking and innovation techniques to challenge assumptions, create, and test an entirely new business concept.

2. *Colliding perspectives*: Understanding the perspectives of people with different perspectives and backgrounds from one's own challenges our mental models and existing mindsets. Leaders who seek colliding perspectives ensure that they continually span boundaries to build an ecosystem: customers, stakeholders, activists, employees, youth…, the more diverse the exposure, the better!

3. *Reflection and sense-making*: By asking powerful questions and engaging in reflection, leaders can develop a broader worldview about what digital transformation can and should accomplish. This is achieved by embracing a growth mindset and deliberately making time for learning from experiences through self-reflection, in-depth debriefs, and action planning.

Interdependent leadership and vertical development go hand in hand. Addressing hidden beliefs and solving complex problems can only gain forward momentum through collective action. The process of vertical development is so important to developing digital capabilities that CCL has embedded it in our client work to develop digital leaders. The global mining case study presented in Chapter 9 illustrates how leaders engage in vertical development as employees collectively move toward creating a sustainable mining company.

Psychological Safety Revisited

In Chapter 2, we discussed some of the fundamentals of psychological safety for the senior leadership group. This concept forms the bedrock of the digital leadership capability model. Digital transformation impacts nearly every function in an organization and involves the work of many individuals, teams, and ecosystems. Because of its central importance to digital transformation leadership — in fact, all leadership — we will discuss additional practices for creating psychologically safe technology teams.

The concept of psychological safety — what it means and how to establish it — has changed over time. In 1965, two researchers coined the term and noted that it was a critical component of the "unfreezing" process required for organizational learning and change and focused on the perceptions and impact of individual workers (Schein & Bennis, 1965). Thirty years later, Amy Edmondson defined psychological safety as "a shared belief held by members of a team that the team is safe for interpersonal risk-taking" (Edmondson, 1999). The concept continues to evolve, particularly in light of digital transformation teams, with Timothy Clark defining it as "increasing intellectual friction while decreasing social friction" (Clark, 2020).

The people engaged in digital transformation work *must* feel psychologically safe to express their perspectives. Duena Blomstrom, in her book *People Before Tech,* presents a compelling case for the role of psychological safety in technology teams (Blomstrom, 2021). She exhorts leaders to recognize and address the "human debt" that has been created in the relentless pursuit of new digital technologies and offers this definition of psychological safety for our digital transformation teams:

> We define a Psychologically Safe team as "A team that feels like family and moves mountains together. One where it feels like they are making magic together — they are speaking up, open, courageous, flexible, vulnerable, learning, unafraid, and having fun together in their bubble

while having a sense of accomplishment about their exceptional performance."

How can digital leaders at any level create psychological safety? We explore four practices to do so:

Tell and retell the story behind the strategic mandate: Emphasize both the need to create financial value for the organization *and* human value. Help the team understand why the organization has embarked on this particular DT journey. Emphasize that while metrics like margin and market share must be achieved, the work required to attain those goals cannot be at the expense of critical concerns like safety, privacy, or equitable human outcomes. Use storytelling to create the compelling change story of why the transformation needs to happen, to help individuals and teams see the future and willingly commit to getting it done.

Set a fail-forward mentality: The DT team will encounter unknown obstacles. Timelines will be challenged. Team members will find themselves needing to shift direction. To counter the urge to play it safe, DT leaders should ensure teams can voice their concerns, offer help, and establish that together, you are on a learning journey. Risk-taking needs to be both encouraged *and* managed: What can we learn from this failure? What would we have done differently? Always communicate that you have team members' backs.

Facilitate dialogue: Ensure that everyone has a voice and balance the dialogue across team members from different functions, roles, and social identities. A rich understanding of these diverse perspectives will be necessary for success because each team member holds a piece of the DT puzzle. Encourage dialogue that explores different approaches to issues and ensure the team has the opportunity to express ideas for *both* innovation and risk mitigation.

Don't assume. Measure: Take the time to measure psychological safety. A simple survey with seven items developed by Edmondson can be deployed with any formal or informal team to understand whether team members feel psychologically safe. Items include questions like "Members of this team are able to bring up problems and tough issues" and "It is difficult to ask other members of this team for help." Aggregated, the measures provide a view of the overall psychological safety and where vulnerabilities exist. Note that feelings of psychological safety may shift over time, so consider remeasuring when major shifts in team composition or project goals occur. When looking at the overall team scores for psychological safety, pay attention to the scores of individual team members. Although the team may score fairly high on psychological safety, some team members may express much less psychological safety than others. Research by Wormington and Loignon notes that the data patterns may illuminate areas where the team may be "fraying at the psychological edge" (Wormington & Loignon, 2022). This fraying may mean that some team members feel that their particular perspectives cannot be voiced or will not be heard. That's a huge loss, as the DT leaders will miss the diverse and critical perspectives required for interdependent work.

The DT Leadership Capability Model

We've discussed three important foundations for developing digital leadership capabilities, including continuous learning, vertical development, and psychological safety. With this foundation, leaders can begin focusing on developing the specific DT leadership capabilities that will foster organizational digital readiness. The Digital Leadership Capabilities Model includes nine capabilities that fall into three cycles of digital transformation, defined as follows:

1. *Understanding the landscape*: Explore the future together, engaging with stakeholders, partners, networks, and teams to create a richer, more diverse understanding of the environment. Understand digital capacity and what capabilities will be needed

to shift the organization. Developing these capabilities will help leaders engage in the digital sensing that prevents periodic disruption and illustrates why continuous learning and an open mindset are so important to digital leadership. This component of the cycle of digital leadership emphasizes exploration.

2. *Translating the possibilities*: Think together, assessing the full impact and risks of decisions; hold and manage the tension between competing priorities and opposing viewpoints. Build open and inclusive relationships to collaborate, share ideas, and solve problems with empathy and compassion for stakeholders. In this cycle of digital leadership, team members must arrive at a decision.

3. *Realizing transformation*: Recognize that digital leadership requires new pathways to personal transformation, transforming the way one thinks and leads. It requires a shift in purpose and identity to impact what one does and how one behaves. Adopt intentional ways of interacting with internal and external partners, span boundaries, empower teams, and encourage confidence and resilience in change. In this cycle of digital leadership, team members must act to transform.

To lead and participate in this three-phase cycle, DT leaders will need to develop nine capabilities. These capabilities are illustrated in Figure 2 and described in the following.

Evaluate the Environment: Assess readiness and identify needs through ongoing evaluation of the digital environment: the digital sensing discussed in Chapter 2. Be savvy to shifts in the market and technologies, and ensure the organization has established customer listening posts — external and internal — for potential opportunities.

Development activities: Identify global thought leaders and engage with them. Find virtual or in-person immersion opportunities.

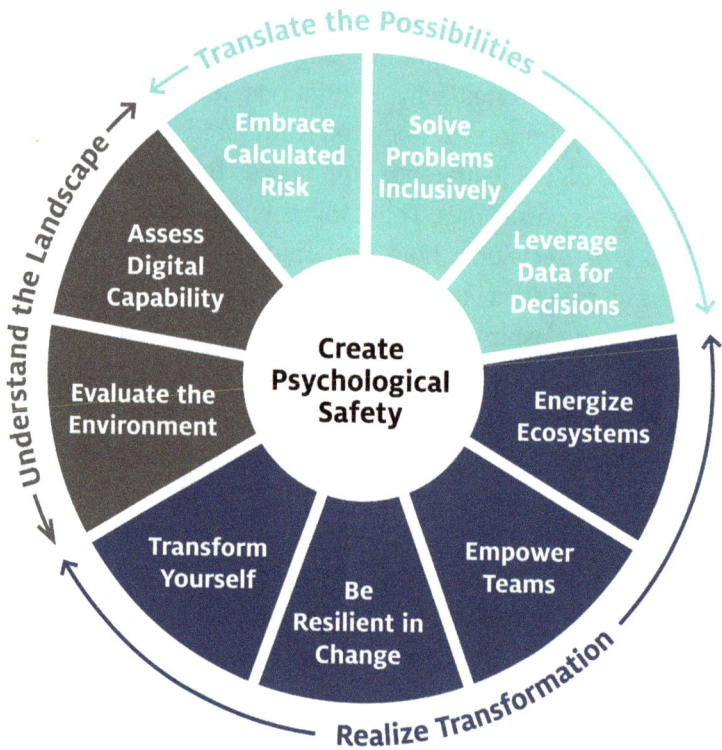

Figure 2:   Digital leadership capability framework.

For example, in DT programs at CCL, global leaders visit leading global digital companies to learn about their business models and transformative leadership. Ensure that digital transformation team members have a funnel of information about market shifts and take the time to read, discuss, and understand them. Leaders must have market foresight and create future fluency to remain competitive.

Assess Digital Capacity: Consider and compare the self, team, and organization in terms of digital strengths and weaknesses. Is the organization actually ready to take on digital transformation initiatives? Does it have the will and the skill to achieve the outcomes, and where are the gaps?

Development activities: Conduct a formal assessment of digital readiness. (In Chapter 5, we offer a digital readiness assessment model.) Engage in process or business simulations. What technology platforms will be touched, and what must change? Is the potential disruption worth the potential value? Where possible, benchmark the potential pain and gain against other internal digital transformation initiatives or those of competitors. Above all, ensure that everyone who will be touched by the initiative *participates*.

Embrace Calculated Risk: Demonstrate risk tolerance and use a calculated approach to taking on risk when adopting new methods. Assessing risk and calculating the potential for success must happen at multiple levels of the organization: those who will create and implement the digital technology, customers, partners, and the communities that will be impacted.

Development activities: Use design thinking to map out all touch points and integration points. What systems will be affected and what is the scope of potential changes? What assumptions will be made about the intended users, and what potential negative consequences could occur?

Solve Problems Inclusively: Adopt innovative, flexible, and inclusive approaches to problem-solving. Individual leaders may not have the right answer, but the collective does. Encourage flexibility and generative dialogue. As above, use techniques, such as design thinking and liberating structures to ensure inclusivity.

Development activities: Listen, listen, listen. Honor diverse perspectives and involve stakeholders from inside and outside your organization. Ensure that the voice of the customer comes first and that all those stakeholders who will be impacted by potential negative consequences have been part of brainstorming potential solutions. Simulate risk mitigation strategies using if-then scenarios. Collective thinking and effective dialogue between all parts of the leadership collective are crucial. Ask many questions. Various scholars and contemporary authors have written about the importance of asking why five times, the use of reflective questions, and agile approaches. Dialogue includes feedback, and we encourage using CCL's SBI model (Situation, Behavior, and Impact) to have courageous conversations.

Leverage Data for Decisions: Be comfortable with incorporating data and metrics into decision-making. Your gut (or the CEO's) is not enough. Data can identify opportunities, e.g., process efficiencies, hidden customer needs, or delivery failures. Critically, data can be used to predict the potential return on an investment, and that includes both the financial and human ROI.

Development activities: Request that relevant data be identified and used in understanding the current state and modeling the ROI of your investment. Use data to set objectives and key results for teams so they know how success will be measured: a critical step toward aligning your team. Use data to test hypotheses for digital innovation, ultimately to abandon or implement decisions. Ensure that data used for machine decision-making result in equitable customer outcomes and do not perpetuate biases based on specific social identities like race or gender.

Energize Ecosystems: Excite and galvanize others, inside and outside the organization, around the possibilities that technologies may bring. A great story of the *why* behind an initiative and the way it is communicated can rally a swell of support. Without it, pockets of resistance are sure to occur.

Development activities: Start with the story of why: the purpose, credibility, and impact of digital transformation. Ensure ongoing conversation circles where employees can share their ideas and be part of collective sense-making. Ensure those communication channels are inclusive. Seek out the influencers and the quiet, unsung heroes who have "been there forever" and know the many potential ramifications of change that you might not. Talk with people who are highly networked and can be your best friend or worst enemy in driving change. Be active in soliciting their help; don't just wait for the survey to come in.

Empower Teams: Act as an encouraging and enabling team leader. You will want to pay special attention to conveying the strategic mandate; determining whether there is direction, alignment, and commitment across the teams; and managing the polarities specific to DT teams (see Chapter 4). Ensure that teams can share their perspectives and encourage honest and courageous dialogue about the challenges and risks those perspectives surface. Above all, empower team members to work in an agile fashion. Pay close attention to team well-being and work-life balance, as digital transformation often requires extra effort and longer hours.

Development activities: Ensure that teams have a clear mandate, tools, and support for working differently and for achieving balance. The mandate should include clear goals and objectives and — more importantly — criteria for new ways of thinking *together* and new ways of working in teams. Tools may range from agile approaches to collective problem-solving to how to create effective communication. Support can range from having the right reward systems that reinforce constructive teaming to advanced practices for integrating remote workers.

Be Resilient in Change: Show belief, confidence, and resilience in your ability to tackle large-scale change on a personal, team, and organizational level. Digital transformation is an ongoing process and a long-term endeavor that demands constant renewal and reinvention. To achieve long-term goals, leaders will need to model the ownership and accountability for successes and failures, coupled with a consistent belief in the journey. By strengthening individual leaders' resilience, the organization emerges stronger, more resourceful, and capable of meeting current and future challenges.

> *Development activities*: Leaders can strengthen resilience and adaptability to change by practicing the capabilities described in this digital leadership framework and implementing the ongoing cycle of understanding the landscape, translating the possibilities, and implementing transformational practices. At the core of this particular capability are self-awareness, self-confidence, and belief in purpose.

Transform Yourself: Practice learning agility and adopt a growth mindset. What we need to know today will not be what we need to know tomorrow. Just as the world of digital technology is constantly evolving, so must you. Digital leaders need to act as role models of personal transformation.

> *Development activities*: Proactively set aside time to learn. Foster your own learning, focusing on both skills and your own preconceived notions, biases, and models of working. Critically, consider how your focus on doing well needs to change to account for doing good. Learn and study the potential negative consequences of digital technology for your team, organization, customers, and the communities in which you work (see Chapter 6 on the societal impact of DT). Take time to reflect on the why of your decisions and whether it's the right why.

Human-centered digital leadership requires that we shift from the development of technological skills and capabilities toward human-centric skills and capabilities. Changing ourselves is the hardest work we will do, and yet, to lead differently, to create a better future that benefits the individuals, organizations, and communities we serve, we must embrace that change.

Key Takeaways and Actions

(1) Invest in developing the foundational leadership skills needed to create interdependent work:

- Adopt a growth mindset and invest in learning. The people you lead need to see that you are investing in your own growth. Learn about new technologies, explore models of digital leadership, speak with customers, and learn about the human impact on the teams that are creating and deploying technology. Extend that learning to include understanding the potential unintended consequences of that technology on vulnerable groups.

- Absolutely commit to creating a psychologically safe environment. Create a safe space, encouraging team members to "take space and make space." Ensure that all voices are heard so that risks and opportunities can be vetted and you are encouraging diversity of thought within the team.

- Engage in vertical development. Use the framework of heat experiences, colliding perspectives, and deep sense-making to hone your complex problem-solving skills. Unearth the hidden beliefs within yourself and others that can derail digital transformation and prevent the organization from realizing its vision of ongoing strategic renewal.

(2) Develop layers of digital leadership across the organization, using a systemic approach:

- One individual leader cannot change a culture. Leadership is a collective social process, and so change requires a systemic approach. Organizations must invest in a process for developing DT capabilities at multiple levels across the organization. We have proposed a DT capabilities model composed of nine capabilities that organizations can use as a systemic approach.

- Individual leaders can prioritize the capabilities they want to develop. Within the chapter, we have provided development activities for each of the nine capabilities. Scaling human-centered digital leadership capabilities across the organization will set the stage for organizational digital readiness.

Conclusion: The Human-Centered Approach for Individual Leaders

To lead in this new world of rapid technological change, digital transformation leaders will need to prepare themselves for the extraordinary and novel complexities this shift creates. As human-centered leaders, they must engage in *continuous learning*, fostered by the *vertical development* required to address the complexities of both doing well and doing good. Leaders can work toward building organizations that *work interdependently*; a command and control orientation simply will not result in organizations that are digitally ready. *Psychological safety* thus becomes critical and fundamental within and across teams as we surface, vet, and address the complexities of digital transformation.

The capability model for individual leadership emphasizes three general leadership capabilities and then builds on them by identifying nine specific skills required to identify possibilities, create the transformational strategy, and actually implement it.

In Chapter 4, we explore some of the inevitable conflicts DT leaders will encounter when they work with formal and informal teams. We present four critical goals that the teams and organization will need to achieve in order to execute and scale digital transformation as a process of strategic renewal. And, we introduce the concept of polarities: a central tension that must be balanced in order to achieve those critical goals.

Chapter 4

Formal and Informal Teams: Managing Polarities and Spanning Boundaries

Acme Energy's senior leadership group has worked with the organization to create a transformation mandate: Reduce electricity consumption by 25%. The transformational mandate has been tied to specific profit goals with a clear story of how the organization can contribute to the UN sustainability goals on climate change. The organization has rallied around this goal, which ties to both doing well and doing good. Informal teams have begun working on a variety of initiatives ranging from innovation and ideation to prototype testing to executing existing projects. Individuals across the organization find themselves working together in new ways and with people they have never worked with before. One informal team has taken on a project to investigate personalized digital services to its customers that also encourages energy-saving habits. Industry best practice research shows that benchmarking an individual customer's energy usage against the customer base can influence customers to conserve energy. The team agrees that this would be a customer-centric approach to achieving the goal and begin working on the idea. Team members focused on innovation speed ahead, only to find that the data governance and privacy protection team has locked energy usage data down as private and secure — and is reluctant to provide access.

Introduction

The cycle of digital leadership — understanding the landscape, translating the possibilities, and realizing the transformation — requires working with a collection of individuals that morph and change as digital transformation takes place. Digital transformation leaders will almost always lead networks of formal and informal teams that span hierarchies, functional boundaries, expertise, external partners, demographics, and regional locations. Each stakeholder will bring to the table perspectives based on their expertise, lessons of experience, process approaches, incentives, and vulnerabilities. Individuals may be evaluated on achieving seemingly opposing goals, and they will have varying levels of familiarity and engagement with the DT project. The DT leader working with this montage of people must develop a team that works interdependently across the organization with the goal of executing and scaling the transformation mandate. It's tough. It's challenging. And it's rewarding. Fostering interdependent work across the organization is a human-centered approach that will create organizational resilience and digital readiness (Figure 1).

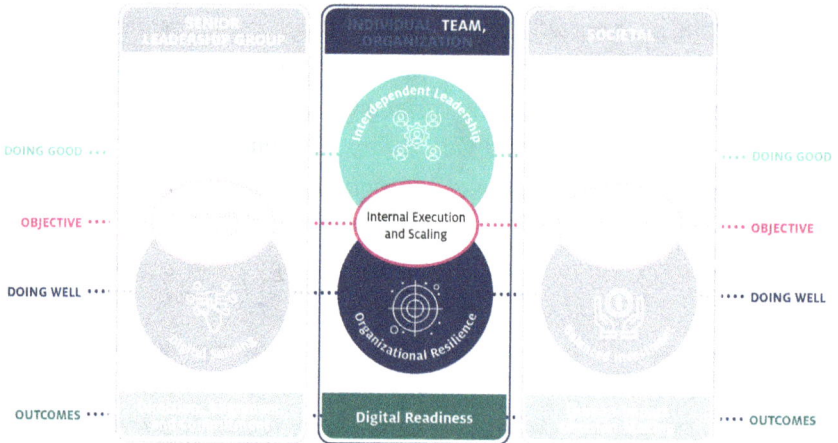

Figure 1:   Internal execution and scaling: Developing interdependent work.

In this chapter, we explore four goals that are critical to successful digital transformation initiatives. These four goals emerged through conversations with digital transformation executives as well as reviews of academic and business literature. And while these are not the *only* goals for interdependent work, they certainly pose significant challenges to digital transformation leaders. DT executives highlighted that while attempting to achieve the four goals, leaders and teams often struggled with seemingly opposite approaches to achieving those goals. Both viewpoints were valid and necessary. However, the differing approaches created tensions that could make it difficult to achieve the four goals.

We can see an example of such tension playing out in the scenario at Acme Energy. The goal is clear: Create customer-centric solutions to reduce energy consumption by 25%. However, one group of team members defines "customer centric" as innovating new products based on data. Another group defines "customer centric" as protecting customer data and managing security breaches for the organization. Both must happen for the project to be successful: There is a central tension, or polarity, that must be managed. In the following section, we define the concept of polarities and then examine how polarities impact the achievement of four critical goals for digital transformation.

Polarities Defined

Polarities are unsolvable tensions. They represent dilemmas that contain seemingly opposing forces, but both forces are necessary and must be balanced in order to achieve a goal (Johnson, 2011). Polarity thinking is *not* problem-solving, which often focuses on either-or thinking. Instead, polarity thinking is characterized by both-and thinking. As a simple example, imagine the strategic objective of achieving a specific margin target. In considering tactics for achieving that objective, you might ask the following question: *Should I focus on topline revenue growth or cost containment?* Your answer will almost certainly be *I need to do both*. This tension between growth and cost containment defines a polarity. Focusing on topline growth may require capital investment, while a focus on cost containment may demand a leaner organization. Thus, to attain the goal of increased profit, the organization must balance the polarity of cost containment *and* capital investments. Both will need to happen to achieve the goal; they must be balanced.

In general, polarities share four characteristics. They are:

- Sets of interdependent pairs that seem contradictory but in fact support each other over time;
- Ongoing with no endpoint;
- Unsolvable;
- Contain two points of view, and both are correct.

As organizations pursue critical goals to become digitally ready, these tensions, or polarities, will show up, particularly when the poles become unbalanced. When one pole receives more weight and attention at the expense of the other, warning signs will appear. These warning signs will often reflect the human vulnerabilities that emerge as information teams begin working interdependently. DT leaders can use the concept of polarities to identify the tensions that may get in the way of interdependent work and adopt human-centered leadership principles to address them. Let's take a look at the four critical DT goals and their polarities. (The appendix provides a full image of Polarity Maps®.)

The Four Critical Goals of Digital Transformation

Figure 2 presents the four critical goals of digital transformation and the central tension that must be balanced in order to achieve the goal. These include the following:

Customer Centricity: Balance agile innovation and seamless integration.

CUSTOMER CENTRICITY			
Left Pole	**Agile Innovation**	**Seamless Integration**	Right Pole
HIGH-PERFORMING TEAMS			
Left Pole	**Productivity**	**Well-Being**	Right Pole
AGILE DECISION-MAKING			
Left Pole	**Centralized**	**Distributed**	Right Pole
TECHNICAL LEADERSHIP			
Left Pole	**Hiring Skilled Talent**	**Upskilling Current Talent**	Right Pole

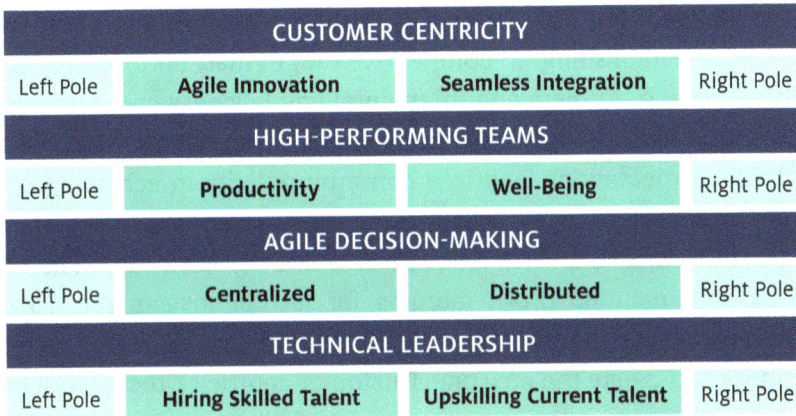

Figure 2:   Four critical goals of digital transformation.

High-Performing Teams: Balance productivity and well-being.

Agile Decision-Making: Balance centralized and distributed decision-making.

Technical Leadership: Balance hiring new talent with upskilling current talent.

In the following section, we explore each critical goal and its central polarity. We introduce polarity mapping as a way to identify both the values for each pole in attaining the goals as well as example warning signs when those poles become unbalanced. This mapping can assist DT leaders in creating interdependent work. We have also included verbatim quotes from our conversations with digital transformation leaders that illustrate why they consider these particular goals important and how unbalanced polarities can slow progress. Finally, we provide human-centered leadership practices for bringing the poles back into balance.

Customer Centricity: Balancing Agile Innovation and Seamless Integration

Digital transformation leaders emphasized repeatedly that customer centricity is *the* focus of digital transformation. DT leaders acknowledged the importance of digital transformation for two goals: (a) establishing a competitive edge that both keeps and acquires new customers and (b) maintaining business continuity that delivers on existing business and expands relationships. These dual customer expectations lead to a common polarity in achieving customer centricity: agile innovation *and* seamless integration. Organizations seek to both innovate and leverage past capital investments and maintain profit margins for further investment. To be customer centric, interdependent teams must both run the current business and create the new one. Customer centricity, then, has a key polarity between agile innovation and seamless integration. In our conversations with digital transformation leaders, they described this polarity in these ways:

> *If you're too loose with the security controls, you could have a data breach. Or if you are too tight with the innovation, you're going to have stagnation.*

> *The application portfolio, the technology stack, the business models, the operating models, all of those things combined lead into a transformation. But on the other hand, there are many, many things that CIOs, CTOs, and CEOs now need to really hang on tight to, things like compliance ethics, information security, data security, and architecture. These are becoming tighter control mechanisms where leadership needs to be exercised at the same time.*

These remarks illustrate the necessity of both agile innovation and seamless integration to achieve customer centricity. Table 1 lists the positive values associated with the two poles of agile innovation and seamless integration. Agile innovation is associated with the values of new product revenue, technology modernization, competitive leadership, proactive risk-taking, and speed to market. Seamless integration is associated with the values of trusted data privacy and security protocols, efficient processes and operations, customer satisfaction, proactive risk mitigation, and safety and compliance. Should a DT leader choose one set of values over another? Of course not. Both value sets are necessary to achieve the goal of customer centricity.

Table 1:   Customer-centricity polarity map.

Goal: Customer Centricity		
Polarity to Be Managed	**Agile Innovation**	**Seamless Integration**
Values	• Revenue from new products • Technology stack modernization • Competitive leadership • Proactive risk-taking • Speed to market	• Trusted data privacy and security protocols • Efficient processes and operations • Customer delight with current delivery • Proactive risk mitigation • Safety and compliance
Warning Signs	• "Workarounds" of corporate policies • Undocumented AI • Privacy or security breaches • Rogue technology or shadow IT • Customer attrition as they defect to more stable competitors	• Rigid approval processes • Data locked down with little access • Excessively constraining requirements for coupling legacy systems with new technology • Customer attrition as they defect to more innovative competitors

Table 1 also includes the warning signs for when the poles become unbalanced. In the case of customer centricity, the warning signs that appear when agile innovation is emphasized over seamless integration (or vice versa) stem from two overarching drivers: the absence of a commercialization engine and the ability to swiftly adapt the match between speed of innovation and business adoption.

• *Absence of a commercialization engine*: Innovation teams can be highly productive in generating new prototypes but hit a brick wall when it comes to commercializing them. DT leaders must think downstream about the impact on business models, current data and technology platforms, implications for organizational structures, and customer support models. Failing to understand these touch points and the cultural implications may be the single greatest cause of failure for DT initiatives.

- *Match between speed of innovation and business adoption*: The business needs and development of technology capabilities may operate at different speeds. Technology changes may occur faster than the adoption of new business models. At the same time, business needs may outpace an IT team's ability to deliver. Traditional teams that lack basic data literacy skills may work more slowly than digital teams. A poor match between the pace of digital advancements and business adoption can create negative consequences for organizational culture.

These two vulnerabilities can significantly impede or even cause the organization to fail when it attempts to execute and scale the transformational mandate. When the organization tilts too far toward agile innovation, the organization may risk teams that create workarounds to avoid compliance with corporate policies; undocumented AI and privacy or security breaches may occur; and rogue technology may pop up out of nowhere. On the flip side, when the balance tilts too far toward seamless integration and business continuity, the organization may risk rigid approval processes and data access that slow down innovation, steep thresholds for demonstrating compliance, or attrition from customers who are tired of waiting for the promised new technology. Be aware that this is particularly likely to happen when individuals are incented to deliver on seemingly competing goals. Again, remarks from digital transformation leaders are as follows:

There is a person who actually needs the world to operate predictably because they are measured or valued around repeatable results, and they have conflict with somebody who is rewarded for disruption. [Managing this] takes a lot of situational awareness and emotional EQ.

The innovators in the organization, like marketing and sales, are trying to move the company forward, the security department in the organization and the leadership around security, trying to prevent any new technology being introduced into the system. They're worried about potential breaches and exposure of customer data. So there's this push–pull around who's making these decisions, and it's frustrating on every level to the people [who] are trying to advance the company versus the people [who] are trying to be protective of the company.

Practical actions for balancing the poles: Interdependent work and boundary spanning

Human-centered DT leaders can balance the poles between agile innovation and seamless integration in two ways. First, always begin with psychological safety. Do all members of the team feel safe to voice their ideas, challenges, and concerns? Second, recall that fostering interdependent work is a foundational leadership skill and critical to creating internal scaling. So engage the stakeholders and team members in identifying the required interdependent work and ask them to share their values and perspectives. Research by Mikalsen, Moe, Stray, & Nyrud provides a useful framework for interdependent work that will help the team express the values and warning signs for agile innovation and seamless integration as they work toward customer centricity (Mikalsen *et al.*, 2018). The researchers identified three types of interdependence that help team members understand one another's work and perspectives:

Outcome interdependence: What goals and rewards motivate the team? The technology team wants the opportunity to stretch their technical prowess and possibly file patents. The data governance team wants to ensure that the algorithm gives customers fair access to policies. Discussing how *both* goals can be achieved will be critical to how the teams support one another and their agreement on how data should be used. For example, directly addressing this interdependency will set the norms for how the teams respectfully navigate data access and use.

Means interdependence: What expertise can be leveraged across the teams? Do some data governance team members have expertise in building AI algorithms? Do some technology team members have specific expertise about existing platforms that support data privacy? What resources exist that both teams can leverage to accomplish the goals?

Boundary interdependence: How can the team span the silos that challenge digital transformation projects? The team will need to understand and work together to understand how the new technology fits with the old and what budgets will be needed to move from innovation to implementation.

High-Performing Teams: Balancing Productivity *and* Employee Well-Being

Every digital transformation leader wants to create a high-performing team. However, DT leaders highlighted that their ability to create and sustain high-performing teams was challenged by attempting to balance team productivity and individual well-being. A highly productive team is characterized by the ability to deliver on challenging organizational goals, high engagement, accountability to objectives and key results, and high standards of excellence. Well-being is characterized as being physically and mentally fit and includes the presence of positive emotions and moods (like contentment), the absence of negative moods (like stress and anxiety), and a tendency to judge life positively and feel good (*Well-Being Concepts*, 2018). Individual well-being and team productivity can work together in a virtuous cycle that leads to high performance (Table 2).

Positive values for productivity include on-time and on-budget delivery, goal attainment, and other examples of delivering effectively

Table 2: High-performing teams polarity map.

Goal: High-Performing Teams	
Productivity	**Well-Being**
Values • On-time/On-budget delivery • Goal attainment for DT initiatives • Commitment to excellence • Efficient processes	• High job satisfaction • High retention • Reduced health insurance costs • Reduced sick days
Warning Signs • Burnout and stress • High turnover • Declines in quality of deliverables and solutions • Excessive rework due to inadequate scoping	• Increased headcount coupled with decreased margin • Entitlement • Missed deadlines • Complaints that others are not pulling their weight

to operational goals. Positive values for well-being include metrics like job satisfaction and retention and health care costs. The virtuous cycle of well-being and productivity characterizes high-performing teams.

However, when the poles become unbalanced, real harm can occur to DT team members and the organization as a whole. Too much weight on productivity may result in burnout and stress, extensive rework, questionable quality, and potentially high turnover. At the opposite extreme, too much focus on individual well-being may result in a lack of accountability, a sense of entitlement, missed deadlines, or even squabbling about the use of sick pay or vacation time. Though it *is* possible to weight well-being too heavily at the expense of productivity, it is much more common to see the opposite, pushing productivity over well-being. This push toward productivity creates stress and burnout, and digital transformation leaders clearly see how that pressure impacts their teams:

We've created an electronic salt mine. Technology enables people to be exploited. We are failing to recognize the boundaries of time and that human beings can only do so much with the time and resources that they have.

Self-deception is when leaders concentrate on delivering results. They see people as cogs in the machine to deal with the results instead of seeing [the individual] who also wants to deliver themselves. But she also has a life and personality and challenges in her family life.

These remarks reflect a global reality. In 2019, the World Health Organization officially named burnout an occupational phenomenon, defining burnout as "a syndrome resulting from chronic workplace stress that has not been successfully managed" (World Health Organization, 2019). The WHO characterized occupational burnout as having three dimensions: (a) feelings of energy depletion or exhaustion; (b) increased mental distance from one's job or feelings of negativism or cynicism related to one's job; and (c) reduced professional efficacy. Chronic workplace stress causes real risk for DT teams. They face aggressive timelines where planned sprints can become marathons, resulting in communication breakdowns, work–life balance concerns, and constant demands to upgrade digital skills (Wu, Wang, Mei, & Liu 2020). These digital transformation teams also take enormous risks and fear failing their organizations.

Balancing the poles: Land on the side of well-being

Because organizations already emphasize productivity and push their technology teams so hard, we urge DT leaders to focus on employee well-being. The science is crystal clear that productivity increases with well-being. But adopting this stance and actively emphasizing well-being requires that digital transformation leaders rethink their own behavior, formal written policies memorialize it, and the organizational culture and expectations make it real. Step back and reflect on how you lead and the messages you send. Are you modeling both your own resilience practices and creating the norms and expectations that your team does the same? Do you find yourself working after normal business hours or sending emails over the weekend, inadvertently creating the expectation that team members will respond? Do you subtly message that work is the most important thing and perhaps message that vacations shouldn't *really* be taken or you will let down the team if you do? One digital transformation leader ruefully said:

> *Messaging is more covert. It's like, "I want you to take your vacation. Don't turn on your phone; don't check your email. Go to Hawaii." But the "don't worry about it" message is mixed with "I think we're about to miss our production deadline. We've got a client who's feeling really intense and revenue is really tight, and you know that our competitor just launched a product that we think might actually torpedo us and you know I want you to take a vacation; but I, as your manager, never would."*

Second, make sure not only you as a leader but the organization as a whole supports well-being. Policies, practices, and beliefs must make it safe and normal to work eight-hour days, take vacations, and learn about and adopt resilience practices. Every employee, whether male or female, single or partnered, with or without children, must have time for family, friends, and the leisure activities they value. The cultural support for well-being must be as visible and normal as the push for productivity.

Agile Decision-Making: Centralized and Distributed

Interdependent work requires making agile decisions quickly and with high quality. Given that DT teams tend to span many boundaries within the organization, getting quality decisions made quickly can be particularly challenging. DT teams must navigate at least two decision-making structures: (1) The senior leadership group that has set the transformational mandate and has the overarching authority to design or approve structure, roles, funding, and authorization levels and (2) the DT teams and stakeholders executing and scaling the mandate. The former must provide adequate resources and funding for success and be informed about high-stakes consequences for the brand. The latter must be free to use those resources wisely and have clear boundaries and enough latitude to make decisions as a team. Clarifying these boundaries and facilitating agile decision-making will foster integrating digital transformation as a process, not a project. Again, comments from digital leaders illustrate the following point:

> *We've always been a somewhat matrixed organization, but it is more so now. We have business units, and then these groups called enablers that cut across all the business units. So at any point in time, you could have people who report up three or four different ways in the same meeting. We must be clear about where expertise sits and accountability sits. These are some complex problems. We're still working our way through who has decision rights, and how many people is too many people to be in a room when you want to actually decide something … The worst thing we can do is get slowed down and have our customers move away from us because we're still thinking and talking.*

> *We spend a lot of time talking about empowerment and prioritization. So [we are] trying to push down the ability for people to set really clear goals. A clear north star. How do we trickle that down into each business? We've really flattened the organization … to get closer to the customer, get closer to where decisions are made at a high level versus at the working level.*

Table 3 presents some of the values associated with centralized decision-making and distributed decision-making. Clearly establishing what decisions will be made where, and by whom, can streamline decision-making with objective metrics (what are we to achieve?), budgets, and reporting expectations. Simultaneously, distributed decision-making to appropriate teams with well-established expectations will give interdependent teams the autonomy they need to make decisions that support the goals.

DT leaders have no doubt experienced the warning signs when agile decisions cannot be made because the organization has not clarified what should be a centralized versus a distributed decision. When decisions are too centralized or must conform to a strict

Table 3: Agile decision-making polarity map.

	Goal: Agile Decision-Making	
Polarity to Be Managed	**Centralized Decision-Making**	**Distributed Decision-Making**
Values	• Clear success metrics • Established budgets and authority for expenditures • High trust in decision-making • Transparent progress reports	• Timely decisions with minimal red tape • High team autonomy and support for quickly solving problems • High collaboration across interdependent teams • Timelines are met • Leaders support interdependent team members who are participating in the initiative • Transparent progress reports
Warning Signs	• Revisiting decisions made by distributed teams • Intense scrutiny of expenditures • Insistence on formal stage-gate reviews that do not add value • Stalled projects	• Rogue decisions without clear cost–benefit analysis • Lack of clear accountability • Poor visibility for progress and goal achievement • Stalled projects

hierarchy, recommendations from informal teams can be endlessly debated or revisited. Projects stall. Morale declines. At the same time, when interdependent teams make decisions too independently, a lack of accountability and stalled projects can also occur. And, changes in decision-making authority can run against the grain. Managers are likely to favor established business models and favor protecting the status quo, actively resisting experiments that might threaten the profitability of existing business models. These vulnerabilities, if not addressed, will act as a significant brake on digital transformation.

Balancing the poles: Clarify how decisions are made and who makes them

(1) Ensure that *who* can make *what* decisions is crystal clear. Ensure the right authorization exists at the appropriate levels to make big and small decisions from approving financing to acceptable risk.

(2) Make sure that decisions are informed by data and not driven solely by gut intuition. Data-informed decisions have higher credibility and can cool emotions when everyone can look objectively at information.

(3) Focus relentlessly on achieving the transformational mandate as the guiding principle. Make the high-value decisions that will ensure success and don't waste time on the trivial.

(4) When teams or individuals make the wrong decisions, whether centralized or distributed, don't punish them. Instead, allow them to fail forward, learn from the mistakes, and course-correct. Decisions cannot be agile if people are afraid to make them.

Technical Leadership: Upskilling Current Talent and Hiring Skilled Talent

Organizations place a high premium on technical leadership because it creates significant competitive advantages. A talent strategy that focuses on technical leadership establishes an innovation edge and drives efficiencies and automation in the current digital product portfolio and technical platforms. However, the availability of technical talent appears bleak. According to the World Economic Forum, technological change will require reskilling one billion people by 2030 (Zahidi, 2020), and Korn Ferry predicts that the United States will have four million technology jobs unfilled by the end of the decade (Future of work: The global talent crunch, 2018). To create technical leadership, organizations need a dual strategy of hiring new talent *and* leveraging existing talent.

New talent can seed innovation capabilities and create opportunities for learning between new and current talent. Investing in upskilling existing talent can be a retention tool, boost morale, and create important career paths. When the poles are in balance, there are equitable opportunities to participate in the creation of technology (Table 4).

The warning signs and human vulnerabilities

This dual strategy makes perfect sense. However, managing this dual talent strategy has created enormous tensions for organizations. Why? Because acquiring cutting-edge technical talent familiar with the newest technologies is expensive, very competitive, and can

Table 4: Technical leadership polarity map.

Technical Leadership		
Polarity to Be Managed	**Hiring New Talent**	**Upskilling Existing Talent**
Values	• New talent seeds innovation capabilities • New talent learns and contributes to legacy platforms • High trust and respect between old and new talent	• Talent strategy emphasizes upskilling • Clear investments of resources and time for career development • Equitable opportunities to mentor and innovate • Existing talent works on innovation projects
Warning Signs	• Hiring costs exceed budget • Salaries upend existing pay scales • New technology cannot integrate with legacy systems • High attrition of existing talent • New hires have better opportunities than existing talent	• Slow adoption of new technologies • Emphasis on maintaining old systems • Poor motivation delays acquisition of new skills • Maintenance occurs, but innovation does not • Resentment toward new hires • Lack of respect

create resentment among existing team members. In addition, initiatives to upskill talent may encounter significant practical and emotional barriers when organizations don't provide sufficient time and support.

Conversations with DT leaders illustrate just how difficult and emotional balancing the approach to technical leadership can be. Leaders know that finding the right new talent can be game-changing. At the same time, when they bring new talent in, existing pay curves are often upended, current employees can feel vulnerable, and resentment toward the "cool new hire" may fester. Worse, commitments to upskilling existing talent are often brushed away in favor of deliverables. DT leaders indicated that hiring skilled talent in their organizations is consistently emphasized over upskilling existing talent. Organizations expect that technology workers will get their normal day jobs done *and* keep up with new technology. Too often, existing employees are asked to learn new technologies on the back of their workdays: Getting things done takes precedence over learning. As one DT leader remarked:

> In a technology-driven world, your team needs to be upskilling all the time. Companies aren't necessarily supportive of investing dollars there, or giving their employees time to go and learn, because everybody's trying to move so fast. But that is going to be something that will be a critical issue in the next few years, because the technology gets more and more complex. And our jobs are all oriented around technology, and so if we are not continually upskilling then you can end up with a team that doesn't get you where you need it to go.

DT leaders are also empathetic to the vulnerability of a workforce that is increasingly concerned about becoming irrelevant. The costs of hiring new talent (particularly when those costs upend the current pay curves) and the "cool factor" can cause resentment and slow the development of high-performing tech teams. The constant innovations in technology lead some technology workers to feel they are simply treading water and struggling to remain relevant to their organizations. And, the arrival of new hires with skills in the hottest, latest technologies can set off an emotional firestorm for existing talent who feel even more vulnerable and at risk, particularly when the new hires receive prime innovation assignments.

We work with teams that are enticed by the idea of digital transformation. They want to innovate. They want to drive change but … we also see what the impact on individual team members is; they're afraid that they'll become irrelevant.

But there's also this fear of people becoming obsolete within companies that are building the digital skills. "Hey, I learned how to code in Sequel. And now you want me to use edge computing or this completely different data lake system that doesn't even use Sequel quick queries anymore? Are you just gonna fire me? Should I go off and become a cook, or are you going to invest in me or just hire in new talent?"

Balancing the poles: Land on the side of current employees

DT leaders voiced the many painful decisions they wrestle with in deciding whether to hire new workers or upskill current workers. That calculus has both an economic and ethical component. A healthy collaboration between new and existing workers can attain the positive advantages that both teams offer. How can digital transformation leaders balance the poles? We suggest taking this human-centered approach:

(1) Ensure that the organization formally sets new skill acquisition as part of performance goals and evaluation. Create the policies and norms that value learning and give people the time to do so as part of their normal workweek. Spend time with team members to understand what they want for their careers, and then build the career development model to support them in achieving their goals.

(2) Use the 70/20/10 model for learning that emphasizes on-the-job learning coupled with mentoring and formal training (Gurvis, McCauley, & Swofford, 2016). This framework suggests that 70% of learning occurs through on-the-job experience and challenges, 20% from working with other people, and 10% from formal training programs and classwork.

(3) Rotate assignments so that both new hires and existing employees work on *both* legacy systems and new innovations. This can help with the goal of achieving customer centricity while balancing agile innovation and seamless integration; it also provides opportunities for all team members to benefit from both developing and implementing the technology, providing them with more equitable opportunities.

Key Takeaways and Actions

When DT leaders engage in executing and scaling digital transformation across the organization, they will almost always manage interdependent teams that span hierarchies, functional boundaries, expertise, external partners, demographics, and regional locations. The interdependent work of these disparate groups must accomplish four critical goals: customer centricity, high-performing teams, agile decision-making, and technical leadership. Each of these goals has a central polarity, or tension, that will need to be managed with a human-centered leadership approach:

(1) Customer centricity requires balancing agile innovation and seamless integration:
- Begin with psychological safety. Ensure the team members that their functional expertise and understanding of what's required to execute and scale can be freely shared.
- Help the team span the boundaries of function, hierarchies, roles, seniority, and geography by engaging team members in exercises

to identify the synergies and challenges of three types of interdependent work:

Outcome interdependence: What goals and rewards motivate the team? Where are goals and performance incentives not aligned?

Means interdependence: What expertise can be leveraged across the teams?

Boundary interdependence: How can the team span the silos that challenge digital transformation projects?

(2) High-performing teams require balancing productivity and well-being:

- Digital transformation teams experience extraordinary stress. Too often, organizations emphasize productivity at the expense of well-being. Digital transformation leaders must rectify this by landing on the side of well-being. Employee well-being will promote productivity, creating a virtuous cycle.
- Take a close look at how you message your expectations to the team. Do you email on evenings and weekends? Do you allow customers to demand impossible deadlines and force the team to meet them? Do you subtly message that a vacation will put a burden on other team members? Examine how your behavior messages whether you value employee well-being, and if it does not reflect that value, change it.
- Model well-being and resilience practices. These practices typically group around physical, mental, emotional, and social categories (Ruderman, Clerkin, & Fernandez, 2022). Let team members know you went for a walk over work, took a vacation, or went home at 5:00. Show them that by practicing well-being yourself, you are giving them license to do so as well.

(3) Agile decision-making requires balancing a centralized and distributed decision-making approach:

- Ensure that who can make what decisions is crystal clear. Create a taxonomy that clarifies which decisions are considered big bets that must be decided by or with the senior leadership team. Understand which decisions will impact organizational functions, particularly as they pertain to executing and scaling the organization. Finally, be clear on what decisions can be delegated to interdependent teams and allow it to happen.
- Make sure that decisions are informed by data. Invest in data-driven decision-making skills and work with the team to ensure decisions are credible because they are based on data, not gut instincts or intuition.
- Spend time only on those decisions that will help achieve the transformational mandate. Don't waste time on the trivial or set up artificial gates to making simple decisions.
- Don't punish teams or individuals when they make a decision that doesn't lead to the desired outcome. Neither you nor they have a crystal ball. If the best effort was made to discuss opportunities and challenges and data informed the decision, then take accountability and fail forward

(4) Technical leadership requires both hiring new talent and upskilling current talent:

- Land on the side of upskilling current technical talent. Technical team members feel particularly vulnerable as fast-changing technology threatens to make their skills obsolete. Bringing in new talent can be extremely expensive, upend existing pay scales, and do so at the expense of loyal and committed employees.
- Ensure that the organization formally sets new skill acquisition as part of performance goals and evaluation. However, back up that expectation by creating the opportunities to learn. Developing new

technical skills should not be done on the back of a ten-hour work-day. Give people the time to do so as part of their normal work week. This will clearly demonstrate the value placed on learning and growth.

- Give current team members challenging technical assignments. Assign them mentors to help them achieve their goals. Avoid putting them in a box that says "you only know how to do this, therefore you will only do this." Invest in proper courses that will help them upskill.
- Rotate assignments so that both new hires and existing employees work on both legacy systems and new innovations. This can help with the goal of achieving customer centricity while balancing agile innovation and seamless integration; it also provides opportunities for team members to develop psychological safety through shared work.
- Ensure every technology team member has a written career development path that uses the 70/20/10 model.

Conclusion: The Human-Centered Approach for Leading Interdependent Teams

In Chapter 1, we raised several questions that human-centered leaders may consider as we balance doing well and doing good, including the question "Who will participate in creating the technology?" One answer: A very diverse group of stakeholders and team members that spans many boundaries. Human-centered DT leadership fosters interdependent work among individuals to execute and scale digital transformation. Individuals will be asked to work together in new and different ways; organizational structures and "the way we do things" will be constantly challenged; and human vulnerabilities about roles, job security, satisfaction with work, and span of control will show up. Human-centered DT leaders can mitigate some of these challenges by actively managing the polarities that can impact customer-centricity, agile decision-making, team productivity, and technical leadership.

We've now discussed two of the leadership levels required for internal execution and scaling: the individual leaders who must invest in building their own capabilities and the leaders of formal and informal teams tasked with fostering interdependent work by achieving critical goals and balancing polarities. In Chapter 5, we turn to the last component of internal execution and scaling: Organizational leadership and the concept of digital readiness.

Chapter 5

The Organization: Developing Digital Readiness

Introduction

Digital transformation tantalizes organizations with its promise. Efficiency, speed, innovation, customer centricity, market leadership: All of these potential benefits shine brightly as organizations work to create transformational change. But, many digital initiatives fail or fall short, with some research finding that only 30% of digital transformation initiatives achieve their objectives (Forth, Reichert, de Laubier, & Chakraborty 2020). Why the missed expectations? Because organizations are not digitally ready. This chapter concludes with the last of the three leadership levels required to create internal scaling, focusing on an organization's digital readiness for transformational change (Figure 1).

The organization itself poses another layer of complexity for DT leaders. When executing and scaling the transformation mandate, the organization must continue to do business while disrupting itself. Both continuity and disruption can be achieved simultaneously when organizations are digitally ready because the organization has created the internal scaling and capacities to embrace change, rapidly shifting and morphing as needed to remain competitive. The organization, composed of its senior leadership group, individual leaders, and formal

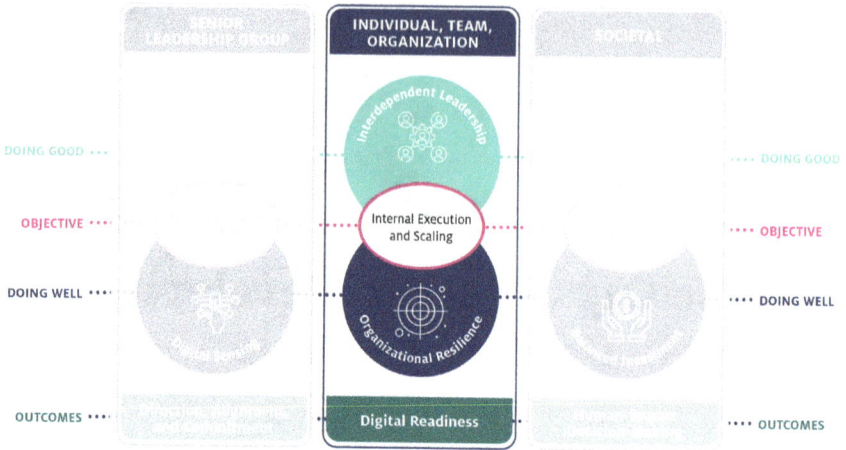

Figure 1:   Internal execution and scaling: Organization readiness.

and informal teams, is becoming resilient through interdependent work. Leaders are becoming ready to implement digital transformation as a strategic process of renewal, becoming an entity that must be agile enough to adapt to technological change through interdependent work.

What does "digital readiness" mean? Researchers Lokuge, Sedera, Grover, & Xu (2019) define digital readiness as *"an organization's assessment of its state of being prepared for effective production or adoption of assimilation, and exploitation of digital technologies"* and is *"both psychologically and behaviorally prepared to take action."* In other words, the organization must have both the *will* and the *skill* to leverage digital opportunities. How can one know whether an organization is ready? What are the strengths it can leverage and the opportunities for increasing readiness?

DT at this level poses one of the toughest tests of leadership imaginable. Every positive and negative aspect of the organization's culture will come roaring to the forefront. The current technology stack (and the people who created it), the technical debt, including the proliferation of rogue IT projects and scattered data, will immediately pose challenges. The organization may be overly protective of data, inhibiting the ability of the new technology to leverage it. It may struggle to scale prototypes into fully functioning production systems. The operations team may be very resistant to learning a new system; they're busy keeping the revenue flowing. All of these potential barriers (and more) can either overtly or covertly create a constant pull toward inertia: the status quo remains in place. Even though the senior leadership group may have created a transformational mandate, individuals have worked hard to develop new capabilities and interdependent teams have reckoned with their different perspectives and polarities, actual change cannot happen without an organizational *culture* that is digitally ready.

Our focus at the organizational level treats the organization as an entity or system with its own unique culture consisting of the shared beliefs, values, and norms that its individual members hold. Does the organization fear the constant change of technical innovation, or do they embrace it with creativity and openness? Does the organization engage in digital sensing, or are they vulnerable to punctuated equilibrium? Do the supports for constant change exist, or are employees in constant chaos, stressed, and burned out? Do individuals perceive threat or opportunity?

> *Digital transformation rocks a lot of people's foundation and there are a lot of power dynamics, overall understanding of what their job is, and the importance and significance of it. There's a huge opportunity and role in leadership to set the stage for what this looks like, and how people become successful in this new world, because there can be a lot of threat that comes across with that too.* — CEO, Marketing Technology

In this chapter, we present a new model for assessing digital readiness based on ten pillars of organizational capacities. Measuring current readiness on these ten pillars will help organizations prioritize which capacities merit investment and create a roadmap for change. At the end of the chapter, we present two case studies demonstrating how organizations have done exactly that in multiyear journeys to transform.

Organizational Capacities for Digital Readiness

How can an organization know that it is "digitally ready"? To answer this question, the Center for Creative Leadership embarked on a research initiative to create a Digital Transformation Readiness Survey (Gross & McCauley, 2020). The early work on this assessment identified ten digital transformation pillars required to realize the promise of digital transformation. The initial topics were developed based on themes from the professional and business literature on digital transformation; our work with organizations undergoing transformation; and insights from our conversations and experiences with DT professionals. The final assessment, an online survey, identified ten pillars of digital readiness, illustrated in Figure 2.

To create a snapshot of an organization's digital readiness, leaders rate a number of statements on how well they describe the organization using a five-point scale. An example question is "We have an inspiring vision of how technologies can enable a new future for the organization," which relates to establishing a transformational mandate. In addition, raters indicate how important that capacity is to the organization. The results can then be used to prioritize a digital readiness capabilities roadmap for systemic change. Figure 2 summarizes the ten digital readiness capabilities, and we follow with detailed explanations of each one.

Let's explore each of the capabilities and implications for doing well and doing good.

Transformational Mandate: *The vision for how digital technologies can enable future competitiveness; a roadmap describing how DT will achieve strategic objectives that deliver business value.* As we noted in Chapter 2,

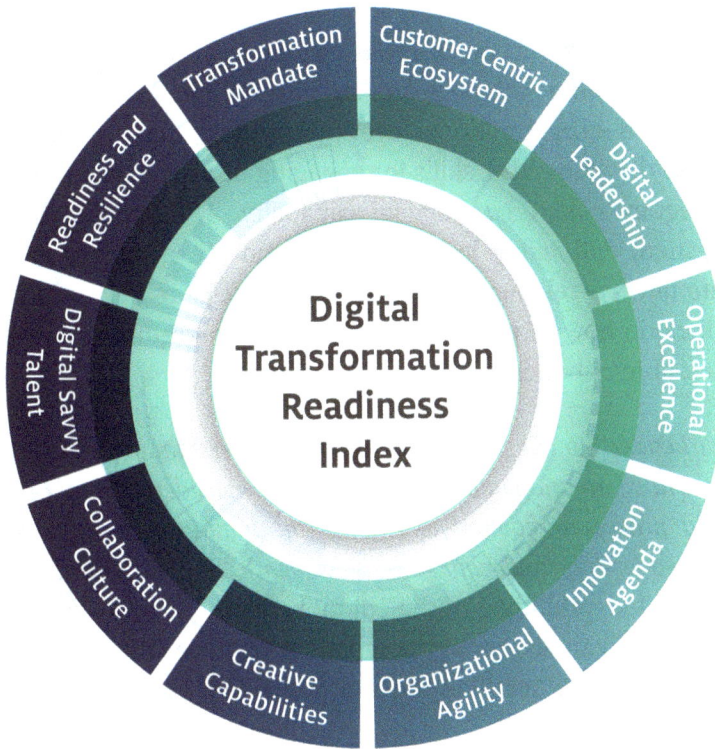

Figure 2:   Ten digital transformation readiness capabilities.

the senior leadership group must develop an inclusive process that results in a clearly articulated transformation mandate. The mandate must have a clear and compelling *why* that speaks to both how it will deliver financial value to the organization and human value, tying to the organization's purpose (Fontan, Alloza, & Rey, 2019). Measuring whether employees believe a transformational mandate has been established is an excellent check on whether the senior leadership group has done its job in articulating that mandate. If the direction is not clear, the organization cannot align and commit to change.

Customer Centricity: Develop market sensing capabilities that provide insights into both customer expectations and engagement; develop an ecosystem of partners, which could contribute to new digital solutions. Effectively use data to build a business case. What does this capability look like at the organizational level? Many individuals in the organization have developed DT skills for engaging in digital sensing, and this now becomes an *organizational* capability. The process has been established, and many in the organization are engaged. Individual leaders have developed their data-driven decision-making skills, and data include how to evaluate both the financial return of investment and the human benefits.

Digital Leadership: Engage leaders in their understanding and support of Digital Transformation initiatives with specific consideration of the human-centered processes required to oversee the initiatives (e.g., governance, change leadership, and change management). The organization has a collective understanding of the components required for a successful outcome. Individuals across the organization have engaged in capability building and understand the interdependent work required.

Operational Excellence: Address the integration of digital technologies that can increase operational efficiencies, including data analytics and/or supporting technology platforms to improve decision-making and coordination. This pillar reflects the capacity for business continuity while disrupting the business. Processes for integrating technology and leveraging previous capital investments are established.

Innovation Agenda: Develop an innovation agenda that encourages all to generate ideas and enables funding models. The ideas add value to existing products and services and enable the monitoring of progress and performance of digital innovation.

Organizational Agility: Develop organizational agility to fast-track digital ideas for rapid execution. This capacity relates to the goal of agile decision-making and whether decisions are centralized or distributed.

Creative Capabilities: Develop creative capabilities hallmarked by inclusivity, learning, risk-taking, and creative problem-solving. Design thinking can be used in working with customers and stakeholders and must address how to solve potential unintended consequences.

Collaboration Culture: Collaborate successfully within and across the boundaries that exist within the organization — be these virtual, demographic, role, function, level, or geographic. The collaboration culture must foster diversity of thought and be open to understanding the cultures and norms of various social groups.

Digital Savvy Talent: Attract, develop and retain digital talent. A human-centered strategy for developing technical leadership must be in place that both refreshes the organization with new talent and commits to skill and capability building for current talent.

Readiness and Resilience: Commitment to overcoming obstacles and barriers. Teams exhibit the ability to deal with changes in direction and willingness to constantly reinvent business models.

Creating a digitally ready organization does not happen overnight. It is a journey, and next, we turn to two case studies from companies that are at different stages of that journey. In the first case study, the organization is in the beginning stages of its transformation journey; the second is several years into its transformation. In each case study, we have highlighted capabilities discussed in the digital readiness model as well as some of the human-centered leadership practices the organizations have put in place.

The Case of the African Retailer

The CEO of a retail company located in an African country had taken over a family business with a proud, decades-old legacy founded on providing products with the best quality and the best price. Brick-and-mortar stores were located in multiple places throughout the country. Customers needed to visit the store to purchase, and the company did not use enterprise software to manage its business. Instead, they managed the business with an array of complex spreadsheets. Although the company had a very loyal customer base and large market share, the CEO wanted to digitally transform the way in which customers purchased and the way in which the company managed its "back office."

To begin the transformation journey, the company decided to implement an e-commerce website to allow customers to purchase online. The site also allowed customers to compare the company's web offers with offers from competitors. However, most customers wanted to see and touch the items they were purchasing, so the website tended to be a place to gather information before viewing the product — customers still wanted to come to the stores. The website slowly gained momentum — though internal conversations continued to challenge the value and utility of this new approach. Simultaneously, the company began scoping and implementing an ERP system that would eliminate the complex spreadsheets and manage the business more efficiently.

After these initial steps, the CEO and executive team realized that "digital" would become a new, future-focused way of operating the business, and the organization would need to invest in that digital future. They had effectively begun the process of digital sensing to be customer centric. The CEO and executive team then reached out to managers in the organization to use the CCL Digital Readiness Survey to identify the strengths the organization could leverage and the areas they would need to prioritize — the beginning of creating the leadership collective and direction, alignment, and commitment (DAC) for the future.

The Digital Readiness Survey showed three key areas of opportunity: Creating a *transformational mandate, developing creative capabilities,* and *attracting digitally savvy talent.* The company acted on this information in several ways. The CEO and executive team clarified the transformational mandate at their annual managers' retreat (the top three tiers of the organization) where the broader leadership team identified, defined, and took accountability for specific digitization initiatives. The "in-flight" DT initiatives for the new website and ERP system were already providing key insights into how this change agenda needed to be led (i.e., giving the mandate to deliver the project as well as focusing on the end-user adoption challenges of any change initiative). Because of a scarcity of digital talent, the company committed to developing its own talent and identified three technologies it wanted for investment: blockchain, big data and analytics, and artificial intelligence. The organization decided to learn about the emerging technologies while simultaneously learning how best to implement these within the organization. The executive team split into three digital innovation teams with objectives to scope and define specific projects in support of the three topic areas. Each team took responsibility for developing the capabilities and technologies for their assigned technology. Each team also selected a leader from the organization and then provided that leader with the budget and authority needed to make things happen and clearly defined metrics for success. To put teeth into the new *decentralized decision-making,* the company barred the CEO and executive team from being involved with these groups, creating *organizational agility.* To begin developing *creative capabilities,* the company invested in design thinking to ensure that the end technology solution was user centric, moving them from a very operations-focused culture to a more *innovative culture.* Ongoing discussions across the organization began to take place in informal and formal ways, for example, at the annual company conference so that all employees could understand the goals and contribute to achieving them: *the collaboration culture* required for systemic change.

The organization remains committed to balancing doing well with doing good. They continue to focus on their critical longstanding value proposition of providing the best quality at the best price with no compromise. They are sensitive to creating an equitable, diverse, and inclusive culture that reflects the demographics of their country. The organization has also committed to developing its existing employees before hiring new talent. Many of these employees have served for years as loyal and valued team members and will receive training and development as the organization works toward digital readiness. Simultaneously, the organization acknowledges that some roles may become redundant as a result of automation. The new guiding principles of the company clearly articulate the focus on customers, the importance of human connection in a digital world, and maintaining the commitment to a long-term digital strategy while executing short-term priorities.

The Case of the Multinational Chemical Company

In this story of cultural transformation in a highly matrixed, global organization, a multinational chemical company needed to leapfrog competition. Its goal? To focus on customer centricity through digitization and connectivity. This organization took many bold steps over multiple years to realize its vision.

First, the organization focused on the story: the why and the expectations for delivery of strategic value. This created the *transformation mandate*. Leaders changed the initial umbrella concept from "digitization" to a seamless customer experience using digitization. They established digital as the enabler and thread throughout that experience and used a continuous communication strategy with podcasts and webcasts to inform and inspire the organization about the new direction. These messages included the company's emphasis on sustainability, "that people are alive and thriving in 2050."

The organization then established a team that focused on creating a *collaborative culture*. This team reported globally and had accountability for workforce education and transforming the organization's acceptance of digitization as a continuous strategic process. How could leaders help the organization grow? What resources would be needed? The team took a strengths-based approach to identify opportunities to collaborate and create synergies.

The company implemented a risky and transformative change through a major reorganization. Leaders realized that the current hierarchical, top-down decision-making processes slowed digital initiatives. To restructure, the company embedded the digital strategy within each business unit by establishing a digital executive. This executive holds responsibilities to both identify digital opportunities within their business units and determine whether these opportunities can be integrated into the overall corporate digital portfolio. The digital executive reports to the global team to create direction, alignment, and commitment. These business unit heads have *decision-making authority* over investments. To make this real, the organization increased its budget from five figures to seven figures for each digital executive. The structure resulted in increased autonomy with accountability to create organizational agility.

This focus on *organizational agility* had an immediate impact. One business unit had struggled with sales, customer retention, and market value. Enabled by the new autonomy, the business unit brought in an outside consultant to create an innovative go-to-market strategy. The resulting event used new marketing digital technology and gamification to create awareness and sell-through for products. Customers responded as they never had before, resulting in eight figures of revenue in a single week, far exceeding historical performance. Without decentralization and the authority, autonomy, and budget to try something new, the region could never have achieved this success.

Operational excellence became critical for this multinational company with multiple operating divisions. Technology had proliferated, and the company inventoried over 250 separate systems being used across the organization. There was no consistent digital strategy to address IT issues. The organization tackled the issue in three ways. First, they focused on what they termed an *interconnected mindset* for systems and people: How do we minimize creating new systems? How do we leverage digital initiatives across multiple business units or platforms? This mindset shift was a first step toward creating interdependent work and a collaborative culture. Second, they convened a multiperson, functionally representative group to develop the vision, pillars, and operating mechanisms for the digital community. Using *creative capabilities* for design thinking, they created a roadmap for change. Finally, the company ensured that the divisional executive digital officer had the latitude to authorize any investments by a business unit or function that aligned to centralized initiatives, always looking to make new initiatives replicable to other groups and integrate with the broader digital portfolio.

The transformation mandate and focus on *customer centricity* have led to a new and evolving innovation agenda. For example, a frustrating and time-consuming manual process for working with small customers will be automated. These small customers often live hand-to-mouth. They need fast access to inventory and fast payment. The organization had competing views about how to approach this: Was it useful to invest in these small clients? Would the organization end up designing a system unique to only one or two of the countries in which it operated? To test ideas, teams from multiple regions convened to create a customer journey map of how a new system would work. Though both teams were convinced that user needs in their regions were so unique that two systems would be required, they ended up with essentially the same map. Duplicate development paths were reduced to one, with configuration, not customization, as the outcome.

This company has realized enormous benefits from its focus on digital transformation, but they are clear that the journey has no end. Challenges remain. Leaders noted, *We have not mastered agility. We have given businesses a lot of autonomy for spending dollars, but what gets in our way is making sure we don't create solutions that cannot be used elsewhere.* And, sometimes the escalation process creates a dependency on hierarchy that can thwart agility.

This company also faces the challenges of team burnout and stress discussed in Chapter 4. To address this, the company began identifying the internal operations and systems that cause frustration and actively reducing those barriers to nurture employee *readiness and resilience.* They have an ongoing process that asks employees "What do you dislike about your job? What are you required to do that does not actually add value? What things might we do that we could automate?" The ongoing process has created a very positive response from the employee base in this inclusive process that focuses on creating human value.

Stages of Digital Readiness

At the end of the day, how do you know your company is "digitally ready"? Perhaps that is the wrong question to ask because being "digitally ready" implies a binary state. In reality, there is no on/off button to say "we are now digitally ready." A digital readiness assessment can help evaluate where an organization stands at specific points in time. However, digital readiness spans a continuum of capabilities and will evolve as organizations adapt their business models to the technological landscape, exactly what we mean by an ongoing process of strategic renewal.

To help describe the fluidity of digital readiness, we have developed a four-level model of organizational digital readiness: Discovering, Adopting, Transforming, and Differentiating. The names in Figure 3 qualitatively describe each level, with special emphasis on

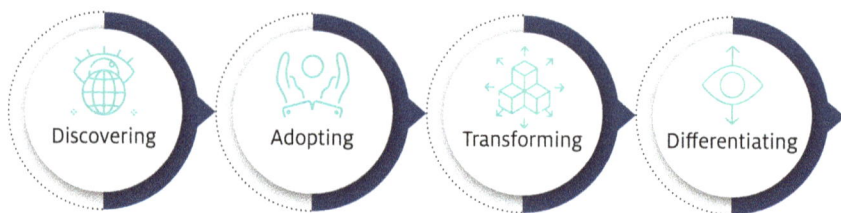

Figure 3:   Stages of digital readiness.

how the organization recognizes opportunity, the formality of business case evaluation, support for both innovation and implementation, and leadership capabilities.

Level 1 — Discovering: Introducing digital technology as a strategic priority is in its early stages. There may be awareness of digital megatrends (e.g., cloud, big data, and AI) and some views of how these affect market dynamics and evolving consumer behaviors in the industry. Leadership has not yet focused on defining digital opportunities for enhanced business impact, or coordination of efforts to create a digital vision and roadmap is limited. Similarly, there may be low levels of organizational alignment and commitment to support digital transformation. Innovation may happen as an isolated practice, and the mindset to support innovation (agility, risk-taking, and iterative execution) is not commonplace. There may be some digital enablement (automation) of processes that create efficiencies and build the foundation for Level 2.

Level 2 — Adopting: The organization has most likely initiated digital transformation to gain a competitive advantage. The case for change and prioritization of investments may be built by individual businesses or functions, and the development of digitally based processes and products will take place in silos. Similarly, transformation may be driven by experiments or projects that are largely within silos; or, test-and-learn approaches to champion innovation may be centralized. Online digital presence supporting consumer activation is expected.

Digital leaders may act as leaders of change in select areas and typically require more empowerment. There is some digital talent within the organization, and several digital activities may be outsourced. Discussions are taking place about how digital transformation can create human value and/or have unintended consequences.

Level 3 — Transforming: There is a pivotal digital transformation strategy in place, supported by partial or organizationwide delivery to scale digitization and digital innovation. Digital success factors are agreed upon and outcomes are cascaded as clear objectives, with a structured recognition framework to reward achievements. The organization is evolving toward customer and employee centricity. Organization structures are flexible and agile. This is supported by behavior as well as digital capabilities to collaborate cross-functionally. Culture change is driven by inspiring digital leaders who have a clear sense of the change strategy and model required to further transform the business. There is a tie to corporate purpose, and the doing well, doing good story is clear, credible, and compelling.

Level 4 — Differentiating: The organization has an enterprisewide digital business model or platform *and* is able to continually reinvent its digital business. Leaders stay current so that digital models are tested and reestablished on an ongoing basis. This is supported by a transformative purpose and a culture of innovation. A digitally enabled consumer and employee focus is part of everyone's DNA, supported by the integration of disruptive technologies to allow seamless collaboration and create distinctive user experiences. Agility underpins the organization's design and operating models, with the capacity to collaborate systemically internally and externally within structured ecosystems. The inclusive and distributed culture is led by digital role models and game-changing leaders.

In the case studies, the African retail company evaluated itself as being Stage 2, while the multinational chemical company evaluated itself as being Stage 3.

Key Takeaways and Actions for Organizations

(1) **Assess your organization's digital readiness:** Participate in an organizational digital readiness assessment that scans the perspectives of individual employees or teams across the entire organization. You will then know where the organization stands on ten digital readiness capabilities.

(2) **Identify which capabilities must be strengthened and take action:** Don't do the capability scan and then do nothing. Develop a clear plan to tackle prioritized capabilities and have the courage to make the big changes that may be needed. Perhaps the organization will need to restructure to foster agile decision-making. Perhaps you will need to invest in building out capabilities for individual leaders. Perhaps you will need to focus on how individuals, teams, and networks collaborate. Identify the gaps and address them.

(3) **Ensure the innovation agenda includes discussions of how technology will do well and do good:** The transformation mandate should have clearly stated how digital transformation is intended to create both financial value and human value. The technical innovation agenda must include deliberate discussions of how those two goals will be achieved. Now is the time for the team to think through questions about who is represented in the data, the benefits and potential unintended consequences of the technology, and how to mitigate them.

Conclusion: The Human-Centered Approach for Organizational Digital Readiness

The DT readiness model and the actions taken in the two case studies illustrate how human-centered leadership practices come to life in digital transformation. Yes, there is a technology component. But more importantly, the model describes how people will work interdependently to create a digitally ready organization. Each company has taken bold actions that were difficult and sometimes controversial. Decentralizing, assigning responsibilities for digital success to a single decisionmaker, a keen focus on customers, disciplined and continuous communications using numerous channels, and investments in people development all underscore the human-centered approach these organizations took in developing digital readiness capabilities. Note that none of these capabilities are about technology itself. Rather, the story is about enabling the organization to execute and scale digital transformation as an ongoing process of strategic renewal. The organization itself must be resilient, and that means changing the way we lead.

We've now completed our discussion of the three DT leadership levels (individual, team, and organization) that must execute and scale digital transformation. In Chapter 6, we discuss DT leadership at the societal level. Organizations will face any number of choices as they evaluate the capacity for their new technologies to create financial and human value. We highlight the potential unintended consequences of technology, the "unseens" that can impact humans, and use the framework of sustainability to engage in human-impact decision-making and whether we are balancing doing well and doing good. We then lay the groundwork for creating an ecosystem of public and private partnerships to make balanced investments guided by human-impact decision-making.

Chapter 6

Society: Unseen Consequences and Human-Impact Decision-Making

The board of a company that creates sophisticated digital platforms for global organizations faced a dilemma. The company, backed by private equity, would be going up for sale in a relatively short time period. High growth had been spurred by an innovative business model that catapulted deal sizes from an average of six figures to seven, and proof points of the new business model were critical for a high valuation. A seven-figure deal was on the table with an eager and highly known brand. But the customer was in a business that many people find distasteful: Though not illegal, the products were known to impact users' health. The board debated whether the sales team should continue with negotiations and sign the highly lucrative contract. Their views considered many inputs. Some members noted that many private equity companies would object to the presence of this company in the portfolio. Others noted the absolute importance of the proof point to a high valuation, which would create a great deal of value for employees and shareholders who had worked diligently for four years to reach this moment. Others reported that the tech team was intrigued by the opportunity to use their technology skills to solve a challenging problem. Others objected because of ethical concerns with marketing and health impacts of products manufactured by the organization. Back and forth it went. What would you do?

Introduction

In 2022, Larry Fink, the CEO of BlackRock, issued his annual CEO letter titled "The Power of Capitalism." He made a provocative statement:

Capitalism has the power to shape society and act as a powerful catalyst for change ... When we harness the power of both the public and private sectors, we can achieve truly incredible things (Fink, 2022).

Powerful words, indeed, from the CEO of one of the world's most influential investment companies. Why do these words matter to digital transformation leaders? Both the access to capital and increased focus on environment, society, and governance (ESG) concerns have increased the pressure to balance doing well and doing good. In this last component of the Human-Centered DT Framework, we propose that organizations must create financial value through balanced investments while achieving positive human value, and we have framed that human value in the context of ESG. Balancing doing well and doing good means organizations will decide how and whether to create and deploy new technologies based on evaluating both the potential for wealth creation as well as sustainable opportunities for global citizens. This decision-making process requires the ability to convene and solicit the input of an ecosystem of stakeholders who can provide diverse perspectives on human impact (Figure 1).

ESG: A Catalyst for Creating Financial Value

At the start of 2020, global sustainable investment reached USD 35.3 trillion in five major markets, a 15% increase over the past two years (Hutchinson, Maher, de Laubier, & Charanya 2022). Investors want to maximize their returns, and there is overwhelming evidence that organizations that pay attention to ESG concerns have higher returns than those that do not. Investors not only focus on ESG

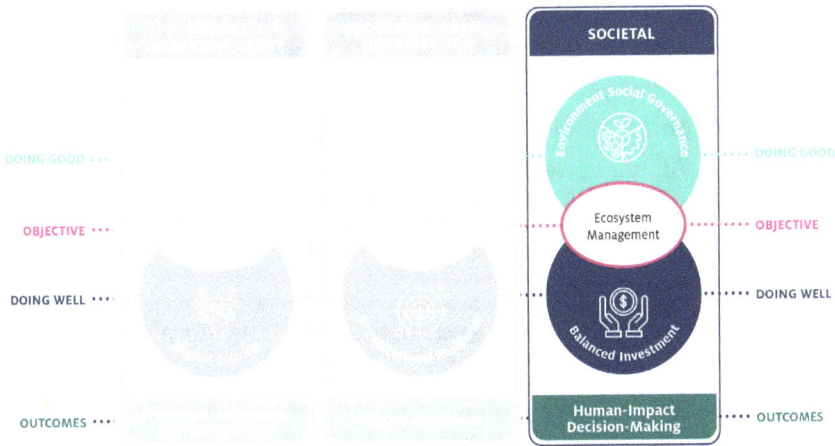

Figure 1:   Human-Centered DT Leadership Framework.

because of that potential for higher returns but because it is the right thing to do as humanity faces the major crises of climate change, an increasing socioeconomic divide, and the threats of digital surveillance and social media.

This focus on humanity's future has catalyzed the collaboration of nations around the world, resulting in several historic global partnerships: The Paris Agreement, the United Nations Sustainable Development Goals, the Task Force on Climate-Related Financial Disclosures, and the United Nations Environment Programme Finance Initiative. These historic agreements are notable because they establish the norms and expectations for what "doing good" looks like within specific timelines. For example, the 2015 United Nations Sustainable Development Goals were adopted by all United Nations member states. The goals include 231 indicators and 169 targets to be achieved by 2030 — a roadmap of expectations for how organizations can balance their investments to collectively create a better future for humankind.

These global ambitions and norms have caused a ripple effect, creating market forces that impact investors, regulatory bodies, customer expectations, and industry collaborations at regional levels. These trends are forcing organizations to pay much greater attention to how they balance their investments so they create *both* financial value and human value with visible proof. The Global Sustainable Investment Alliance defines four such trends that illustrate the increasing investor emphasis on organizational accountability to doing good (2020).

- *Market Drivers*: Both retail and institutional investors have shown increased interest in companies with a focus on ESG. In addition, the availability of new global financial instruments and norms for evaluating ESG have created new reporting mechanisms and expectations for transparency.
- *Customer*: The interest of individual investors in ESG has resulted in new types of investment instruments. These individual investors are demanding that their monies be used responsibly not only to create wealth but to create a more sustainable world, addressing key issues, such as climate change, health and safety, environmental violation, corruption and bribery, water and food security, and employment security.
- *Policies and Regulations*: Every region of the globe has governing bodies and regulations focused on mitigating harm, or better yet, optimizing the impact of corporate growth strategies and digital transformation. Examples include the 2018 European Union Sustainable Finance Action Plan, the US 2021 Executive Order on Climate-Related Financial Risk, and the 2020 Guiding Opinions on Promoting Investment and Financing to Address Climate Change in China.
- *Industry Collaboration*: Specific industries or groups within each global region have made calls to action, resulting in public commitments or even specific products. For example, in 2020, Canadian universities launched the Investing to Address Climate Change Charter; over 120 investors and organizations in the US endorsed

the Investor Statement of Solidarity to Address Systemic Racism and Call to Action created by the Racial Justice Investing (RJI) Coalition, and Africa released the African Green Bond Toolkit to guide how to issue green bonds that align with international best practices and standards for ESG (Figure 2).

These global agreements and market trends are incenting organizations to show their commitment to ESG, and the resulting commitments often have a specific tie to digital transformation. One in four companies reports that ESG is the primary focus of their digital transformation initiatives, with 80% focused on social goals, 70% on governance considerations, and 69% on environmental programs (Hutchinson *et al.*, 2022). The pressing need to create global environmental sustainability and greater socioeconomic equality for all people has galvanized investments in technology and digital transformation.

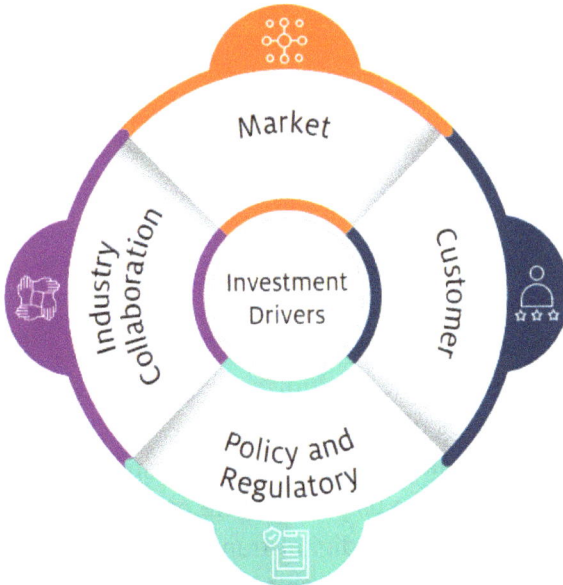

Figure 2:   Drivers of ESG investing.

This energy and commitment are laudable. However, our aspirations for a sustainable and equitable future will be derailed if we do not identify and mitigate the potential negative consequences of digital transformation. We must manage the "unseens." To do that, we need to be aware of what those unseen consequences are and ask hard questions about how we will contribute to or mitigate them as we deploy digital technologies.

Unexpected Consequences and the Unseens

In a series of global Expert Round Tables (ERTs), multidisciplinary scientists conducting research on digital transformation gathered to discuss the impact of digital transformation on humanity. The ERTs convened in Japan, Europe, South America, India, North America, and Africa to discuss the key digital transformation categories (e.g., economic change, environmental systems, and cybercrime), the intended impact, and the potential unintended negative consequences (Scholz *et al.*, 2018). The conversations and statistical analyses resulted in a thorough taxonomy of the specific negative consequences of digital transformation, described as "unseens."

The ERT participants clearly recognized and affirmed the opportunities for digital transformation to do good. However, they also outlined in vivid language and illustrations the harm that digital transformation can cause. Human-centered digital transformation leaders must be keenly aware of these unseens and factor them into the development of digital technologies. We have organized a subset of the unseens discussed by the multidisciplinary round tables into the overarching categories of ESG.

These unseen negative consequences are specific to digital transformation and should give us pause as we consider the fair and equitable use of technology. As digital transformation leaders, we hold responsibility for considering these questions:

Environmental: *How do we protect a global environmental ecosystem that no longer easily rebounds?*

Societal: *How do we avoid exploiting vulnerable people?*

Governance: *Who makes decisions about how data is generated, consolidated, owned, processed, and shared?*

As you peruse the "unseens" of digital transformation, we invite you to reflect on the above questions in the context of your organization: What is the organization attempting to accomplish with digital transformation? What discussions have been held to truly vet the unseen consequences, and who has been a part of those discussions? Questions like these will form the basis for how an organization decides to invest in and implement digital technologies.

Environmental unseens

Sustainability: We have depleted the Earth's resources. Water has become a scarcity, which threatens crop production, leading to fears of massive famines. Trash floats even in the deepest recesses of the ocean. Fires rage. Developing countries do not have equitable sources of energy, while developed countries consume far more than their fair share. Committing to sustainability has become a high-stakes, very public strategy as organizations collaborate to save planet Earth. The ERTs recognized this existential threat and called out two impacts from digital technology that specifically contribute to that threat:

Increased energy consumption and waste: Digital facilities required to store, retrieve, process, and transmit data require energy and physical hardware. While digital data consumption has increased, the technology and systems to mitigate the environmental impact of that consumption have not. Electronics quickly become out of date, demand for rare minerals (e.g., cobalt for electric vehicles) has increased, and some technologies like cryptocurrency consume vast amounts of energy. Although DT aspires to *reduce* energy consumption and waste, it also *increases* energy consumption and waste. The puts and takes may not cancel one another out, let alone lead to a reduction.

Barriers to the circular economy: Digital technology also aspires to create a circular economy where materials are shared, leased, reused, repaired, or recycled for as long as possible. Increased consumer demands for digital technology increase every aspect of production, from packaging to distribution to end-of-life. Bringing the circular economy to life has been very slow. The resulting waste has a disproportionate impact on poorer countries that have built industries based on waste disposal.

Societal unseens

The digital economy — The right to participate: Digital transformation is widening the gulf between the haves and the have-nots. In fact, some economists propose that the established definition of gross domestic product (GDP) as based on labor, capital, and resources has fundamentally changed and must now include digital data. This radical shift in our understanding of the economic impact of digital transformation creates a heavy responsibility for DT leaders. We must be aware of the unintended consequences of creating a digital economy that excludes many humans.

Access: About one-third of the world's human beings do not have access to the internet and are generally found in the poorest, most populated countries. Without access, these humans cannot participate in the digital economy. And, simply having access is only the beginning of crossing the digital economic divide: Physical components, smart components, and connectivity components are required as well. Assuming ubiquitous access leads to the unintended consequence of leaving behind almost a third of the world's population. How will networks be expanded to ensure opportunities for all?

Digital literacy: Access is only one barrier to participating in technologies intended to benefit people, like telehealth or electronic banking. Public entities and governments increasingly rely on digital delivery of programs, information, and services. Governments are investing in smart cities where public services like transportation and health care rely on digital connectivity. Digital services require some digital savvy. New technology intended to expand accessibility and improve efficiency may leave behind significant numbers of people who do not have familiarity with digital technologies. How will vulnerable people obtain access to basic services if they do not know how to use the digital technologies that govern that access?

Irrelevancy: Each industrial revolution has created demands for new skills, disrupting the economic well-being of the current workforce. Digital transformation's impact is no different. Routine, task-based work is being replaced by AI and robots. Tasks that currently require cognitive processing and decision-making by knowledge workers will *also* be replaced as AI algorithms become more sophisticated. "Labor" is being fundamentally redefined. What happens, then, to the Amazon warehouse worker? The Starbucks barista? The paralegal?

Being human — Emotion and well-being: How can technology satisfy our needs for human connection? Although digital transformation is intended to connect us to other humans, it can distance us by pulling individuals away from satisfying and deep relationships with others. The virtual world can create the illusion of connection without the emotional satisfaction required for well-being.

Fragmentation of life and cyberaddiction: Technology demands that we pay attention. It is designed to be immersive. But the unseen consequences of designing for immersion are the fragmentation of life and cyberaddiction. The constant pull to engage and interact with social media, gaming technologies, advertising, and even online learning inadvertently means that humans attempt to multitask … the email ping that distracts us from a conversation with a friend, the text advertisement that pulls us away from work. These distractions can result in a loss of efficiency and affect well-being. The "hooks" built into social media like scarcity (information only available for a short time) and reciprocity (inviting friends to join a platform, making it harder for individuals to leave) can create compulsive behaviors. Fear of missing out, presence features, and other designs make it hard to disconnect. How do we draw a line between immersion and compulsion?

Seeking connection with robots: Artificial intelligence aspires to automate the mundane, freeing humans up for greater creativity, deeper relationships, and satisfaction in our lives. But in some cases, social robots take the place of humans. Some take the roles of conversation partners, while others are caregivers. The Japan expert round table identified a trend in Japanese culture to glorify humanoid robots, attributing capabilities to them that might not be real. In recent years, a Japanese citizen went so far as to marry a gaming character. Robot caregivers for the elderly have become reality. In some experiments, humans have relied more on the advice of robots than their fellow humans. Is it sufficient to replace our need for human connection with connection to a robot?

Digital etiquette: Forums for discussion have moved from the in-person town hall to online sound bites on Twitter, WhatsApp, TikTok, and other social media. Cancel culture creates fear that saying the wrong thing will make one irrelevant. The patchy, inhuman communications create less empathy and relationship trust. Cyberbullying has led to increased suicide, particularly among teenagers. How do we foster authentic human communication using digital technologies? How do we protect vulnerable youth from harm?

Governance unseens

The transition to a digital economy has made the governance of data one of the most hotly contested topics of the 21st century. Humans generate data that touch nearly every aspect of our individual, organizational, and societal lives. Inappropriate use of that data creates unseen impacts that imperil our right to privacy, democratic institutions, and unrestricted access to information.

Governance over data and digital technologies

Data privacy: Data generated by humans powers the digital economy. Most individuals provide that data in a willing exchange — my data for your technology. However, unseen, negative consequences happen when that data is no longer secure, perpetuates bias, or is used without consent and transparency. For example, there are pending regulations in some countries that would force voluntary DNA testing results to be shared with insurance companies, raising questions about how companies would use that data to evaluate risk and set insurance rates. The reversal of Roe v. Wade in the US has caused many women to stop using apps and platforms that collect their health information for fear of reprisal, even though these apps provide beneficial health information to the women who use them.

Data compensation: Corporations reap enormous wealth from the data provided by individuals. Consumers have begun to question whether they should be compensated for providing that data. Big data based on DNA, health trackers, and buying habits — virtually everything obtained online — can be used by corporations in creating financial value. To what extent should citizens be allowed to monetize their own data?

Data oligarchies: Enormous industry players like Google, Apple, Meta, Amazon, and Microsoft have made such profound technology innovations that thousands of organizations have opted to use their platforms for data storage, information exchange, and algorithms to create knowledge from that data. Certainly, a potential unseen is the impact of a large-scale security breach or use of the data in cyberwarfare. Another unseen is the impact on small- and medium-sized businesses that may be shut out of participating in the digital economy and may have valuable technical and regional expertise that can enhance the success of a digital initiative.

Political polarization: Social media began as a way to connect and inform. The manipulation of data and information to create fake news threatens democracy as humans fall prey to the disinformation campaigns that have disrupted society. AI algorithms, based on preferences, continue to serve up information that corroborates current views, seeking additional clicks and engagement rather than a robust representation of the issues. The perpetuation of false information makes it difficult for citizens to discern truth and make balanced decisions based on their values and beliefs. How do we mitigate polarization?

The AI digital curtain: Decision-making

Biased data: Stories about the consequences of using biased data to create AI algorithms haunt the digital transformation industry.

Creating an algorithm from one group and applying it indiscriminately to another group can perpetuate biases and cause real harm. For example, these algorithms can determine the attributes of beauty, estimates of health and life span, and gender and race categories based on facial recognition. How do we ensure the use of inclusive data that mitigates bias, and how do we unwind algorithms based on data with existing bias?

Digital vaulting: Data and digital environments now comprise a layer between humans and their environments. The algorithms serve up what information we see, how that information is contextualized, and what information means have become automated. The machine-based computational layer creates those decisions. Who determines whether the algorithm is "correct?"

Managing the Unseens

Are we asking digital transformation leaders to solve all the world's problems? Yes and no. We are asking that as human-centered leaders, we become aware of the opportunities and potential unintended consequences of technology. We are recommending that as DT leaders engage in digital sensing, we include identifying opportunities to contribute to ESG and UN sustainability goals. We are recommending that DT leaders ask provocative questions that cause the organization to think differently about what is possible. And, we are specifically asking that DT leaders deliberately design and engage a stakeholder ecosystem that guides digital transformation decisions using a human-impact decision-making framework.

Human-Impact Decision-Making Frameworks

In the opening scenario of this chapter, the senior leadership group of an organization debated whether to engage with a client whose industry posed some ethical challenges for investors, employees, and customers. At the same time, the new technology and contract mechanism developed for this client would represent a leap forward in the organization's business model. The organization believed that proving this methodology could create a substantial monetary return for loyal and hard-working employees when the company acquired new investors.

Unfortunately, the organization arrived at this decision point without established guidelines for making the decision. There was no existing process or framework to discuss and weigh the conflicting needs and perspectives: the responsibility to employees who had invested years in building the company and expected to financially benefit from that investment, the potential impact on the brand in working with the client, the ability to obtain new venture financing, and the impact on the humans buying the client's products. Some of the emotions and friction over the decision could have been mitigated if the organization had established the *a priori* principles that would guide discussion and decisions. A clear statement that "we do not work with companies in these industries" or "these are the steps we will go through to determine whether we will work with certain clients" would clarify whether the situation had a clear-cut decision based on guidelines, and if not, the process the organization would use to evaluate human impact. This situation is absolutely not unique. Many, if not most, companies do not establish these guiding principles before encountering such dilemmas. Stakeholders can work together to establish a decision-making framework for evaluating the impact of digital technology on humans.

What might such human-impact decision-making framework look like? Research scholars in the field of digital transformation have begun proposing various models of ethical decisions. Corporate Digital Responsibility, the American Computing Machinery (ACM) code of ethics for software development, works on Value Sensitive Design, journals like *Ethics and Information Technology*, and the book

Ethical Machines by Reid Blackman are all examples of emerging ethical frameworks for the creation and use of technology. The field of artificial intelligence ethics alone has resulted in hundreds of papers, organizations, and journals devoted to understanding, documenting, and warning about the potential ethical issues associated with AI and machine-learning algorithms (e.g., AI Now Institute). These organizations and frameworks are important resources for informing an organization's own framework. However, we propose that these processes and guidelines should accommodate the diverse perspectives of the entire stakeholder ecosystem, one that focuses first on the *process* of making the decision rather than the outcome.

We begin with a process definition developed by researchers Christensen and Kohls: "An ethical decision is a decision in which all stakeholders have been accorded intrinsic value by the decision-maker" (Christensen & Kohls, 2002). An ethical decision is not the outcome itself but rather the process of inviting to the table all the humans who will be involved in investing in, profiting from, co-creating, using, and being impacted by the technology. Stakeholders must include representatives from the communities whose resources will be consumed at various points in a circular economy. Indeed, government representatives, customers, investors, technical experts, social scientists, employees, users, regulators, policy advisors, and community representatives should have an opportunity to be at the decision-making table.

These diverse perspectives must be both heard *and* valued. And to demonstrate that those perspectives are indeed valued, DT leaders must make decisions that honor and support those perspectives as often as possible, landing on the side of doing good. We thus define human-impact decision-making as follows:

Human-impact decision-making is a process in which all stakeholders have been accorded intrinsic value by decision-makers who carefully evaluate options to balance the creation of both economic and social value.

The process of ecosystem management, coupled with human-impact decision-making, gives power to humans who might otherwise be invisible, leading to the unseen consequences that can create human harm and damage an organization's reputation. Brands that establish an *a priori* process for human-impact decision-making can avoid the hasty decisions that can damage brand reputation.

Organizations will be at different stages in creating guidelines for human-impact decision-making. In some cases, regulatory industries set clear guidelines, such as GDPR or the Ethics Guidelines for Trustworthy Artificial Intelligence published by the European Commission in 2019. In other cases, aspirational goals, like the Sustainable Goals set by the United Nations, become guidelines. Specific industry-governing principles can assist in establishing guidelines, such as the value of "autonomy" in health care where every effort is made to respect patients' wishes. Organizations might consider the consequences of working in countries that would benefit from the wealth created by their industry but where human rights are routinely violated. Another approach to developing ethical decision-making frameworks would be reconsidering the expected metrics for determining a product's value. For example, engagement metrics are a standard way to measure the value of a social media application. But should organizations not also question whether social media applications create addiction, increase feelings of loneliness, or create vulnerabilities to bullying? In this case, engagement metrics are inadequate for evaluating *both* financial value and human value. In this context, if the social media application is targeted at youth, then a decision about engagement and content requires that parents and youth be at the table to share their experiences and perspectives.

These considerations for human-impact decision-making will become ever more complex as humans and machines become increasingly intertwined. The definition of "human" interaction, the increasing reliance on AI for decision-making, the increasing technological socioeconomic divide, the right to data privacy, and the impacts on the environment, all of these complex considerations, must be considered. Organizations need to face these questions *now* and will need to proactively establish thoughtful processes and guidelines for choosing how, and whether, to move forward with initiatives that create financial value yet have the potential to negatively impact humans.

In addition to establishing a process and guidelines for evaluating the financial and human impact of digital technologies, the organization's transformational mandate must remain front and center. Ideally, the mandate connects the business model to both its ability to generate wealth and support the organization's corporate purpose. Where the organization chooses to invest its time, money, and resources clearly signals its views on both financial and human value creation.

Take, for example, BP. This oil and gas company is in the process of disrupting its own industry, with over 40% of its capital investments going toward renewable energy and the goal of reaching net zero carbon emissions by 2050. The company also aims to create a "just energy transition" and contribute to the ongoing care of the planet, focusing on biodiversity, water management, a circular economy, and sustainable purchasing. The shift in capital investments backs the words with money and is an emerging example of the balanced investment that takes into account both economic and social impact. Interestingly, BP also emphasizes a stakeholder engagement process that includes commercial partnerships with cities and corporations to help them meet their decarbonization goals. The partnership ecosystem BP has built includes investments in digital technology startup firms to accelerate the achievement of these goals.

In practice, establishing the guidelines for balancing investments to create financial wealth and positive human impact will feel daunting. We pose some practical steps for creating those guidelines:

Codify what you have already decided: Begin by memorializing known decisions. If the organization has already made decisions, e.g., industries they are unwilling to engage with or published ethical codes for AI algorithm development, communicate that. Pay attention to published ethical guidelines and codes of conduct for technologies and industries germane to the organization.

Establish that human-impact decision-making means the ecosystem of stakeholders have shared their perspectives and the perspectives of vulnerable people may be favored in a decision: Be respectful of the lived experiences and wisdom of the people who will either use your digital products and services or be impacted by them and invite them to the table. Consider the disability rights movement slogan, *Not about us without us*. That's a pithy way of saying that policies, decisions, actions, capital allocation, and digital products and services should not be made without the participation of the group being affected. Don't build products for women with an all-male team using data collected mostly from men. Don't build telehealth solutions without understanding whether community members can access, understand, and use the products. Do involve parents and mental health professionals when creating apps for children. These principles may be obvious, but putting those principles into action requires a radical shift in how we design and operationalize products.

Spend time surfacing potential issues: Establish listening posts for the entire stakeholder ecosystem and include them in the digital sensing described in Chapter 2. Hold discussions to understand the potential "unseens," categorizing those unseens and clearly stating the potential consequences. Understand the severity of the unseen impacts on multiple dimensions, including value creation, such as revenue or brand reputation and ESG impact. Consider engaging outside negotiators and mediators like the Consensus Building Institute to help the organization and the stakeholder ecosystem engage in the deep, complex problem-solving required to both do well and do good.

Be transparent and trustworthy: An organization's stated intent to do good — and attainment of those goals and management of the unseens — is highly visible. Clear communication of intent *and* impact will create trust with the private/public partnerships that have vested themselves in the DT initiative's success. For example, Dick's Sporting Goods is committed to stopping gun violence. As a part of that commitment, the company made the decision to stop selling guns. That decision and resulting action required the courage to knowingly sever a lucrative source of revenue. However, in doing so, Dick's Sporting Goods gained value: Despite initially losing $150 million in sales and destroying $5 million worth of gun inventory, stock rose by 14% the following year.

Leveraging the Human Ecosystem

Our process definition of human-impact decision-making begins with inviting a stakeholder ecosystem to the table so multiple voices can be heard. Organizations will need to devise comprehensive process models for how and when to convene stakeholders as they develop their digital transformation strategies. We suggest that organizations begin by creating a taxonomy of stakeholders who will be involved or impacted at each stage of the transformation journey. Although not comprehensive, this list provides some ideas for who might be invited to the table:

- Transdisciplinary scientific experts
- End users of the technology
- Representatives of the communities being impacted
- Customers and end users
- Partners, such as suppliers and distributors
- Industry organizations
- Government regulatory bodies
- Digital transformation policy groups
- Ethics and compliance officers

- Technologists and data scientists
- Implementation and operations specialists
- Community representatives

These stakeholders will offer organizations the multi-lens perspectives needed to be aware of and respond to the market, customer, regulatory and policy, and industry drivers outlined at the beginning of this chapter. More importantly, they can create the *a priori* guidelines that guide human-impact decision-making. We can only understand and appreciate these perspectives when stakeholders are at the table to share their perspectives on the human impact digital technologies will have.

Engaging the stakeholder ecosystem will be critical to managing the unseens and creating both economic and social value. The deliberate inclusion of the ecosystem will be exhilarating and frustrating. And yet, without it, how can we claim that our work balances doing good and doing well, or that we are engaging in human-impact decision-making? We must prepare ourselves to wrestle with these complex issues as we speed toward our technological future.

Key Takeaways and Actions for Managing at the Societal Level

Investors, customers, and individual citizens have increased pressure on organizations to commit to doing good. The availability of capital for growth may hinge on those commitments and our actions to mitigate damage to the global environment, create equitable opportunities for all citizens of planet Earth, and guard against the malicious use of data and technology. This is a noble calling for digital transformation leaders and one that will require fundamental shifts in the way we work. We have recommended some actions to begin this shift:

(1) Make sure the transformation mandate publicly commits the organization to doing good: Tie the organization's purpose to global initiatives like ESG or the UN Sustainable Development Goals. Create purposeful systems of actions and measurements that can show real traction in attaining those goals.

(2) **Establish the processes and guidelines for human-impact decision-making:** Educate the organization on the potential unseen consequences of digital transformation and make it a practice to discuss and weigh those risks as development and implementation procedures. Ensure that process begins with inviting an ecosystem of stakeholders to participate in decisions. Deliberately include those who can identify the potential unseen consequences. Take every opportunity to land on their side.

(3) **Make a purposeful effort to build a robust stakeholder ecosystem:** Researchers, scientists, customers, community representatives, suppliers, and policymakers all become potential stakeholders that should be included in discussions. Deliberately identify the players, thinking through how global locations, functions, scientific bodies, government agencies, and others should be involved. Just as organizations have established the process that governs the ideation, prototyping, development, and release of technological products, so must organizations establish the process of involving these stakeholders in human-impact decision-making.

Conclusion: The Human-Centered Approach to Societal Impact

In this chapter, we made the business case for why a focus on doing good creates financial value. Organizations using a balanced approach to digital transformation attract investors as well as the goodwill of customers and employees. Key trends in ESG have set new expectations for the stewardship of digital transformation initiatives, and investors, customers, and individuals are increasingly placing capital with organizations that demonstrate their commitments and results.

The world needs our commitment to doing good, and digital transformation leaders are uniquely positioned to do so. We can lead differently, shifting to a keen focus on understanding and managing the unseen consequences that can impact our fragile planet and global citizens. We need to deliberately focus on human-impact decision-making and ecosystem management. We need to establish processes and guidelines for weighing the impact of digital technologies that are as carefully considered as the processes and guidelines for creating the technology itself. And, we need to shift toward decisions that land on the side of the stakeholders who have the most to lose.

We have now completed our discussion of the Human-Centered DT Leadership framework. We have examined models of human-centered digital transformation leadership at five levels: The senior leadership group, the individual leader, team/group leader, organization, and society. In the following chapter, we turn to one additional topic before turning to our case studies: Equity, diversity, and inclusion (EDI). We consider this topic of such great importance to creating our digital future that it merits a frank and unflinching discussion. EDI transcends leadership levels and underlies some of the fundamental questions underlying digital transformation.

Chapter 7

Equity, Diversity, and Inclusion in Tech: A Call to Action

Introduction

Who creates and profits from digital technologies? Who is represented in the data used to develop the technology? Does technology create equitable outcomes for majority and minority groups?

No discussion of human-centered leadership would be complete without considering the critical role of equity, diversity, and inclusion (EDI), and this is especially true for digital transformation leadership. EDI threads through every aspect of the technologies shaping the future of human beings. It intertwines with and transcends all models and levels of leadership. Why? Who participates in the development of digital technologies, who reaps the benefits of that technology, the potential bias in artificial intelligence algorithms, and the equitable access to and impact of technology on minority groups shape the human outcomes. It is essential that we step back and examine our stewardship of EDI as we create our digital future.

We begin this chapter by summarizing the business case for committing to EDI as a central component of human-centered digital transformation leadership. We then follow with a sobering picture of who participates in and benefits from technology. We then make recommendations for (a) radical reflection on EDI commitments, (b) resetting hiring, retention, and promotion practices, and (c) raising awareness of the critical role of artificial intelligence. We end with full acknowledgment that while human-centered leadership requires promoting equitable, diverse, and inclusive teams and the development of fair and equitable technologies, individual DT leaders can only accomplish so much. The organizations in which they work must be deeply committed to this challenging and rewarding work.

Why EDI Is Good for Business: Doing Well

Four driving forces have made conversations about race and gender ubiquitous in the boardroom and the *C*-suite, including a looming shortage of technology workers, transparency in human capital metrics and the ability to obtain funding, innovation and diversity of thought, and legislation requiring organizations to be accountable for their impact on marginalized people. Research by the Center for Creative Leadership corroborated the significance of these trends and the impact of EDI on global businesses. In 2019, we asked 500 senior leaders around the globe to identify the three most disruptive trends that would significantly affect their organizations over the next five years (Center for Creative Leadership, 2020b). Digital transformation leaders will not be surprised that the top three most impactful trends relate to technology, including big data and analytics, agile innovation, and artificial intelligence. What might seem surprising was that 33% of these global leaders indicated that EDI would significantly impact their businesses over the next five years. Why did they view EDI as having such a significant impact? The answers lie in three themes:

Increasing acquisition and retention of top talent: Global leaders see a talent shortage coming in the tech sector, and current research findings confirm that shortage. With the looming gap in technology talent and the critical need for technical leadership, organizations will need to recruit, hire, and retain employees by casting a much wider, more inclusive net. And, diversity matters to both employers and employees. A 2020 research study found that more than three in four employees and job seekers (76%) report a diverse workforce is an important factor when evaluating companies and job offers, and that is particularly true for black, Hispanic, and LGBTQ+ job seekers (Glassdoor, 2020). People *want* to work in organizations with diverse and inclusive cultures.

Accelerating innovation and diversity of thought: What new ideas and innovative products or business models might organizations miss because they lack diversity in their innovation teams? Global leaders discussed how diverse teams create better, more innovative technology. Additional research verifies those beliefs. For example, when women are included in scientific teams, the teams are better able to solve complex problems (Badall, 2014), generate higher revenue and profit (Lorenzo *et al.*, 2017), and accelerate revenue from innovative products and services (Nielsen, 2017). As one CCL research participant noted:

> Encouraging greater diversity is not only the right thing to do: it allows scientific organizations to derive an "innovation dividend" that leads to smarter, more creative teams, hence opening the door to new discoveries.

Transparency in reporting and investor scrutiny: The U.S. Securities and Exchange Commission mandated human capital disclosure by all companies selling securities in the United States. Although the SEC did not provide rigorous guidelines for the human capital metrics to be reported, the International Standards Organization issued guidelines related to organizational culture, diversity, recruitment and turnover, productivity, health and safety, and leadership. These guidelines include recommendations for reporting diversity metrics at various leadership levels and at the functional level, including technology groups. Investors continue to pressure organizations to address EDI issues. For example, the Interfaith Center on Corporate Responsibility (ICCR) reported that diversity and racial justice was the most common topic for 2021 proxy resolutions (ICCR, 2022), and from 2018 to 2022, S&P 500 earnings calls tracked a 658% increase in mentions of EDI (Gartner, 2022). Organizations see this and are responding. As one global leader noted:

> *Equity, diversity and inclusion is a thread throughout our strategic plan, it is so important that we have developed a human capital plan that aligns to our strategic plan. We have made it our mission to ensure our leaders are responsible for this part of our culture and have made it a critical element in their performance standards.*

The business case for committing to equitable, diverse, and inclusive cultures, and how this translates into technology development, is very clear. Many organizations have made at least some commitment to EDI values, included it in their strategic plans, and made it a part of their talent strategies. However, despite these commitments, data indicate that we have much more work to do.

Where the Industry Stands

The number of women and people of color in tech remains frustratingly static, despite the recognition by the tech sector that diversifying the workforce creates a competitive advantage and, for some, is a moral obligation. To put it bluntly, technology remains the purview of a relatively exclusive group. Consider some of the statistics: In 2019, only 27% of computing roles and only 15% of engineering roles were held by women (US Department of Labor, 2019). Although $137 billion was invested in over 10,000 US startups, only 1% of those investments went to companies with black founders. And, despite making up 13% of the United States population, black talent represents just 5% of the tech sector workforce. This small fraction improved by only 1% from 2014 to 2020 (Kapor Center, 2020).

Why does change seem so elusive? We have identified two major issues that may stand in the way and offer suggestions for change: (1) potentially biased recruitment, development, and promotion practices and (2) organizations may not be truly committed to change. Catalyzing change begins with DT leaders reflecting on their own beliefs and then actively addressing every step of the talent value chain from recruitment through promotion.

Radical Reflection: Challenging Yourself on Your Own Beliefs and Values

That image of who "belongs" in technology subtly shapes our beliefs and actions. Stop and visualize leaders in technology-driven companies. Do images of Steve Jobs, Mark Zuckerberg, Bill Gates, or Elon Musk pop up in your head? Or images of Ginni Rometty, Marvin Ellison, Roz Brewer, Ken Chenault, Lisa Su, or Megan Smith? When you think about the mathematicians and scientists who contributed to the very beginnings of computer science, who comes to mind? Our images of technology leaders can shape our beliefs about who belongs in technology. Those beliefs can subtly shape our behaviors as we either encourage or inhibit equitable, diverse, and inclusive tech cultures. We need to take a good hard look at those deeply held beliefs and everyday behaviors. That is the only way that real cultural change will happen, and we suggest beginning that process with radical reflection (Ferdman, 2017). Radical reflection can help us identify how our beliefs and practices might prevent us from actively creating a more equitable, diverse, and inclusive culture and is a component of vertical development (Matias, 2018). The following reflection questions are a way to begin, and what you find out about yourself may surprise you.

- **How self-aware are you?** How well do you know your own social identities, biases, and cultural background, and have these social identities shaped how you show up and how you experience the world (Ruderman & Ernst, 2010)? In what settings do you share aspects of this background when working with technology teams? What do you know about yourself and the power you hold over other people because of your social identities?

- **Who and what influences you?** What voices and perspectives are you attending to? When discussing technical issues, does a woman receive as much of your attention as a man? A white person and a person of color? How are you testing the realities of your efforts to create relationships that include people who aren't exactly like you? Look at your network. Does it primarily reflect your own social identities, or is there a montage of diversity across many dimensions? Are you exposing yourself to others' perspectives and experiences?

- **Who is in power?** Why are specific people in power? How are authority and power used within the digital transformation team and the organizational culture? As you examine the hierarchy responsible for digital transformation, be honest about whether this hierarchy reflects your commitment to EDI. What does your tech organization actually look like? What might you need to do to shift power so that diverse voices shape strategy, policy, and execution in digital transformation initiatives?

- **What is considered "normal" or "fair" in the organization?** How do perceptions of fairness maintain advantages for members of some groups over others? How does that show up in who is considered "good" at technology and subsequently is hired or promoted? For example, are assumptions made that "good" technologists must come from Harvard or MIT or Carnegie Mellon? Think about the way in which computing tasks are assigned. Do men typically receive assignments to create the hard-core intellectual property (IP) that might be patentable and women typically receive assignments in quality assurance? If these patterns exist, ask yourself why and how you contribute to those patterns.

- **What internal conversations have you had?** How have you discussed and acted on creating an equitable, diverse, and inclusive team? Have you engaged your technology team(s) in conversations about their concerns and hopes for the culture they want to build and how? Are their ideas being incorporated into your organization's mission, values, design, policies, and norms? How do you know? What positive adaptations might you make to systems, policies, and mindsets that are in your sphere of control? How might you foster greater equity and inclusivity by activating the lessons from your and others' lived experiences and histories?

In Chapter 3, we discussed the concepts of continuous learning and vertical development. Engaging in radical reflection is a part of that leadership development process. The process can help us identify opportunities for change both in our own perspectives and in actions we might take. Toward that end, we turn to some practical suggestions for improving the ways in which we hire, recruit, and promote technical talent. The reflection questions above set the stage for finding areas of opportunity to strengthen committed action toward developing equitable, diverse, and inclusive technology cultures and digital products.

Embedding EDI in Our Tech Talent Strategy

In Chapter 4, we discussed the critical goal of creating technical leadership for competitive advantage. A deliberate focus on finding, hiring, and promoting people representing a wide spectrum of social identities can and should be a critical part of a comprehensive talent strategy. It simply makes good business sense, and it reflects human-centered leadership. However, beliefs and habits for executing that technical talent strategy can limit our opportunities for technical leadership. In this section, we consider three major stages for capitalizing on those opportunities when we focus on EDI:

(1) *Recruiting*: How do we find and select candidates?
(2) *Including*: How do we embrace, develop, and promote tech talent?
(3) *Future-proofing*: How do we create equitable pathways to participate in tech?

To develop the concepts presented here, we begin with a framework presented in a report produced by a working group of practitioners, social scientists, corporations, policy institutions, and other collaborators (Catalyze Tech Working Group, 2021). (The contributors to this working group represent the ecosystem of stakeholders discussed in Chapter 6. If you are inspired to learn more about EDI in tech, and take action, we highly recommend reading this report.) We have added to this framework by including information and recommendations from academic and business literature and digital transformation leaders.

The recruiting process: The recruitment and selection process sets the stage for diversity itself: The actual numbers of people representing various groups. Four actions can help us create more diverse teams: (1) widen the narrow and exclusive tech recruiting process, (2) reconsider job descriptions, (3) ensure a diverse slate of candidates, and (4) manage bias in the selection process.

Widen the narrow, exclusive recruiting process: Bias can creep into our technology talent recruitment processes in subtle ways, beginning with where we look for that talent. We tend to recruit and hire people from our own networks, and our own networks tend to look just like us. This repeated habit defeats our intention to diversify tech teams. Consider the experience of a CPO at a high-growth digital transformation company: *We are committed to diversifying our workforce, especially for our senior teams. However, we have a problem. We have a very influential board member who is a white man. He is wonderful and knows about everything and everyone in our industry. When we have openings for senior team members, he provides recommendations. They are always excellent candidates — but they are invariably white men. Because of his influence, we often end up hiring that person without a thorough recruitment process that creates a diverse slate. That makes it hard to meet our ambition to create a more diverse and inclusive technology team.*

Homogeneous technology teams perpetuate in another way. Because organizations see technical leadership as a competitive differentiator, they seek the "best talent." In the US, the definition of "best" may be narrowly associated with Ivy League schools and top technology universities like MIT, Stanford, Caltech, and Carnegie Mellon (Chua & Mazmanian, 2020). And yes, these schools tend to have more men than women and more white people than people of color graduating with computer science and other technology-related degrees:

> *The myth of talent includes the implicit assumption that only the graduates of a few elite private universities are truly brilliant, talented, and worth hiring. We see this myth in action … when companies hire within a small insular ecosystem of institutions that are wealthy, socially prestigious, and demographically homogeneous* (Catalyze Tech Working Group, 2021).

To cast a wider, more inclusive net, DT leaders can partner with their HR leaders to create a talent acquisition strategy that purposefully and directly connects with community colleges, historically black colleges, female or BIPOC engineering groups, and other organizations. Think beyond LinkedIn. For example, partner with groups like Black in AI. Work with your search firm to ensure they have deliberately worked toward a diverse candidate pool. If recruitment firms rely on homogeneous networks or are themselves biased in their processes for screening candidates, they will miss opportunities to invite minorities to the process. A focus on casting a wider net requires thoughtful, deliberate action, and leaders might need to slow down the process to make it more inclusive.

Carefully examine job descriptions: Job descriptions pose a barrier to recruiting women and people of color for technology roles. Women tend to be drawn to the use of a more communal and interpersonal style of speech than men and are more likely to disqualify themselves from jobs when they believe they do not possess the required skills. Danielle Collier and Charlotte Zhang at Cornell University provide examples of words that appeal more to men than women and the resulting impact on whether women choose to apply for a position based on the job description (Collier & Zhang, 2016).

Engineering company description
- Masculine: We are a *dominant* engineering firm that *boasts* many *leading* clients. We are *determined* to *stand* apart from the *competition*.
- Feminine: We are a *community* of engineers who have effective *relationships* with many *satisfied* clients. We are *committed* to understanding the engineering sector *intimately*.

The use of language in job descriptions/engineer qualifications
- Masculine: *Strong* communication and influencing skills. Ability to *perform individually* in a *competitive* environment. *Superior* ability to *satisfy* customers and *manage* company's association with them.

- Feminine: *Proficient* oral and written communications skills. Collaborates well in a *team* environment. *Sensitive* to clients' needs and can *develop warm* client *relationships.*

Engineer responsibilities
- Masculine: *Direct* project groups to *manage* project *progress* and *ensure* accurate task control. *Determine compliance* with client's *objectives.*
- Feminine: Provide general *support* to project team in a manner *complementary* to the company. *Help* clients with construction *activities.*

Ensure you have a diverse slate of candidates — no excuses: Job descriptions, personal networks, and the universities tapped for recruitment all impact the ability to develop diversity in our technology teams. However, another issue frequently crops up: The slate of final candidates. A study by researchers from the University of Colorado Leeds School of Business found that when a pool of four candidates included one woman and three men, there was a 0% chance a woman would be hired. If the pool of four candidates included two women and two men, there was a 50% chance of hiring a woman (Johnson, Hekman, & Chan, 2016). When hiring technology team workers at any level, ensure that the final candidate slate includes multiple highly qualified women and people of color. Be prepared to combat perceptions of fairness. Quotas or targets can cause controversy, and some employees will believe that the best candidates are not considered for roles when focusing on diversity.

Managing bias in the selection process: Look carefully at the recruitment interview process, where the bias of interviewers can inadvertently impact the process of diversifying technical talent. These biases are many and can be quite subtle. For example, researchers have found that people of color and women are less likely to be hired if they are black candidates with natural hairstyles (Koval & Rosette, 2021), do not fit perceptions of elite social class associated with technology (Chua & Mazmanian, 2020), or are subjected to the "whiteboard coding" interviews that create stress and cognitive overload (Behroozi, Shirolkar, Barik, & Parnin, 2020). Setting clear rating criteria for the role and organizational fit will help interviewers mitigate the impacts of their personal biases.

Beware of using artificial intelligence: Finally, beware of the impact of AI algorithms and machine learning to identify potential candidates. The academic literature is currently mixed on whether hiring algorithms create bias in the selection process, including resume selection and the initial recorded video interviewing process now used by many organizations (Bogen & Reicke, 2018). These algorithms promise neutrality, but proof of neutrality is often provided by the for-profit vendor of those very algorithms. At the very least, when using hiring recruitment software that relies on AI, ask the vendor to explain how the algorithm mitigates bias and monitors results. If the software fails to provide a diverse talent pool and final candidate slate, it's likely biased.

Creating inclusive cultures: Changing the current culture to embrace the perspectives of minority groups requires a purposeful, program-matic process for change. DT leaders acknowledge how important this is, noting that organizations must move beyond "check-the-box" exercises like unconscious bias training or focusing simply on diver-sity metrics. Creating inclusive technology cultures requires that we change our actions so all technology team members have fair and appropriate access to opportunities so all team members are included at every step (Center for Creative Leadership, 2020a).

Projects and task assignments: Who participates in patent applica-tions? What factors lead to new and more prestigious assignments? Too often these assignments go to men, while women take on less prestigious assignments, such as quality assurance testing. The consequences manifest in different ways, from making it more difficult to promote women to fewer patents being held by women to the stock options granted to create wealth. To create inclusive and equitable participation in high-profile product development, project assignments must be equitably distributed and push toward taking on new and prestigious challenges (Holtzblatt & Marsden, 2018). DT leaders can also be mindful of recognizing the importance of *all* work associated with project success. For example, do digital transformation team members developing new AI algorithms receive recognition for their work, whether they are preparing the data, working on quality control, guiding the machine learning, or developing the production code?

Promotion and sponsorship: Who is your next CIO or CTO? If internal candidates are being considered, who are they and why are they being considered? Take a clear-eyed look at how candidates are identified, developed, and sponsored for promotion. Understand the challenges of individual contributors, first-time managers, and functional leaders within technology and develop systems of support that enable them to become more proficient in their work *and* ladder up to the next level (Young, Leslie, Balakrishnan, & Winn, 2021). Do consider establishing mentorship and sponsorship programs for people from minority groups, but lean toward sponsorship. Importantly, ensure that sponsorship comes from highly influential senior leaders and that these opportunities are equitably offered (Ibarra, Carter, & Silva, 2010).

Increasing personal power: Providing feedback, including helpful critiques, clear expectations, and good coaching creates increased personal power. Because a person belongs to a minority group does not mean DT leaders should hold back on providing that feedback, and sometimes they do. Afford everyone the opportunity to learn and grow (Holtzblatt & Marsden, 2018).

Establish accountability: Make responsibility for inclusion part of everyone's success metrics. Expectations and metrics can be built into the performance evaluation process, into technology design processes, and into the cultural norms for discussions. Allocate time for team members to participate in employee resource groups. Set aside time for teams to discuss various EDI topics, books, or articles. Always remember the importance of psychological safety and measure it.

Design with, not for: In Chapter 6, we emphasized that human-impact decision-making means including the stakeholders impacted by the decision in the decision-making process. Similarly, ensure that design processes are inclusive: Those intended to benefit from the design are part of the design team. Developing trust in their knowledge and lived experiences can be a powerful tool in creating an inclusive culture. Those perspectives can also mitigate inadvertent bias in what is created, such as concepts of beauty, appropriate language, and facial expressions (Chang, 2020).

Future-proofing talent availability — A step toward equity: Where does future tech talent come from? With the looming tech talent shortage, we must begin creating equitable pathways for participating in tech. This means thinking beyond the current emphasis on Ivy League and tech-focused universities. For example, almost half of all undergraduates in the U.S. are enrolled in community colleges. These community colleges represent a wealth of untapped talent where we can invest to diversify tech, and organizations are seeing the possibilities. Higher education institutions like George Mason University are establishing new transfer models that make it easier for community college students to successfully transfer to four-year colleges. Tech apprenticeships in New York City, such as those sponsored by corporations like IBM, Barclays, Spotify, Foursquare, 2U, and Stack Overflow, are presenting new opportunities to develop tech engineers (Center for an Urban Future, 2019). Intel has invested in a partnership strategy with Maricopa County Community College to create a two-year artificial intelligence associate degree. Creating equitable pathways for diversifying tech is not an impossible dream, but one that many organizations have invested in to fill the tech talent gap, reap the advantages of more diverse teams, and quite simply, do good.

Small Steps Lead toward Systemic Change

The actions outlined above for creating a more equitable, diverse, and inclusive technology culture are not new. However, a focused, concerted audit of whether a team or organization actually implements those practices might be surprising. Take the case of one tech-oriented team that evaluated its own practices, found opportunities, and took action. The team worked within the context of an organization that was strongly committed to EDI and had developed a strategic plan for cultural change. Within this context, the team took on the task of updating their own hiring, development, and promotion processes. They first looked at where they were recruiting and realized they relied too heavily on traditional pipelines like LinkedIn. The team worked with the HR talent acquisition team to ensure that job postings deliberately focused on historically black colleges and universities. They established connections with engineering and AI organizations that promoted diverse technology talent. Second, they created a new process for evaluating job descriptions, including testing commercial algorithms like Textio and inviting people of color and women to evaluate the job descriptions. The team leader insisted on having a diverse slate with "two in the pool" for any new position and adhered to the policy. The interviewing process established *a priori* criteria for rating candidates, and the interviewing team cut across functional boundaries and was itself composed of a diverse team.

In addition, the team used an inclusive process to create a new career development pathway that established the criteria for promotions and pay increases. Team members, HR representatives, and outside reviewers all participated in developing the document. A final review was made by an expert in EDI, and the review resulted in a major gap. Feedback indicated there were not enough "teeth" in the career development pathway for accountability to EDI. In addition, some language needed to be revised. What was intended to be a "final review" became a more extensive one and resulted in setting metrics and accountability tied to EDI goals within personal development plans, commitments to equitable, diverse, and inclusive data science and research practices, and to improving evaluation systems. Finally, an extensive benchmarking review of pay showed gender inequities that needed to be addressed, and actions were taken to do so. These change steps took a lot of time and energy. The process was slow and sometimes frustrating. However, the work was worth it. The process and resulting career development document became a framework for other teams in the organization. The process for recruitment changed and resulted in a more diverse slate for job openings. Perhaps most importantly, the team and organization benefited from the demonstration of commitment to EDI through the concrete actions and inclusive process.

The Dangers of Biased AI

We cannot leave the EDI discussion without drawing attention to the profound possibilities and consequences of AI technology. We must be more aware of how AI impacts marginalized groups. In the article "Redistribution and Rekognition," the author, Sarah Myers West, argued that AI algorithms are resulting in "algorithmic oppression," stating, "As artificial intelligence systems are deployed around us, they exhibit the same forms of inequality and discrimination that many of us experience in everyday life — only in ways that are more invasive, scale more rapidly, and are much less visible to us" (West, 2020). West reviewed a number of examples demonstrating the concerns. Examples included how Microsoft's AI chatbot learned to use racist language in a single day, the racially discriminant COMPAS system that was two times more likely to label black defendants as future criminals than white defendants, automated decisions that exclude people of color from home loans, facial recognition errors based on skin color, and false claims that AI software could detect fear. These alarms have been raised by many researchers as self-learning algorithms entrench the original biased data in new decision-making algorithms. Reid Blackman, in his book *Ethical Machines*, notes: "… while the ethical risks of AI are not novel — discrimination, invasions of privacy, manslaughter, and so on have been around since time immemorial — AI creates novel paths to realize those risks. This means we need novel ways to block those paths from being traveled" (Blackman, 2022).

Virtually all digital transformation leaders will inevitably work with teams who develop artificial intelligence and machine-learning algorithms. We call upon all digital transformation leaders to educate themselves on how artificial intelligence can exploit the humans it is intended to serve and the best practices that will prevent harm. We have a responsibility to steward the development of AI. This will require constant vigilance, our commitment to learning, and fostering psychological safety within technology teams. DT leaders must educate themselves enough to ask informed questions about the teams developing AI algorithms, holding the team accountable for creating fair outcomes.

Good Intentions and Fragmented Actions

The actions listed above can begin catalyzing change in organizations as they commit to building equitable, diverse, and inclusive cultures. However, no leader works in a vacuum; they only work within the context of their organizations, and not all organizations are ready or willing to engage in this challenging work. Consider the brutal murder of George Floyd. The video depicting nine minutes of police brutality galvanized protests around the globe. Business corporations rushed to respond as people united to demand action. CEOs considered how to answer that call as they weighed both brand and personal reputations and the credibility of their commitments. Thus began a flood of public responses to answer the call to action. Corporate statements came from the world's biggest tech companies like Amazon and Apple, manufacturing companies like Caterpillar, and financial institutions like Bank of America. The CEOs clearly supported racial justice, but did they create a clear roadmap for how their organizations would address their own cultures or invest in racial justice initiatives?

This question became the focus of research conducted by the Center for Creative Leadership. Members of CCL's Leadership Research and Analytics team analyzed the corporate statements issued after George Floyd's murder. Statements included those from Fortune 100 companies and from members of the CEO Action Network for Diversity & Inclusion. The team examined more than 202 statements representing 228 organizations (Dawkins & Balakrishnan, 2022). The researchers found that corporate statements about commitments to EDI fell into three categories:

- *Cosmetic*: Primarily a public relations or compliance tool.
- *Conversation*: Stories and experiences shared with psychological safety to promote learning.
- *Commitment*: Indicator of concrete, sustainable action.

The analyses indicated that an astounding 95% of corporate statements were cosmetic. The statements lacked the key details and commitments that indicated organizations planned to create long-term culture change. In other words, though organizations identified EDI as both critical to their success and a moral imperative, they struggled to fully commit to change and define the actions they would take.

Why does this response matter to human-centered leadership? Because if the organization itself has not seriously committed to creating an equitable, diverse, and inclusive culture with clear goals and tangible actions and resource allocation, then it will be difficult for DT leaders within the organization to do so. In Chapter 2, we discussed the critical importance of creating a transformation mandate that results in the direction, alignment, and commitment of the organization to that mandate. The organization's commitment to EDI must have that same clarity. Statements must become an actionable roadmap to systemic change, promote sincere conversation across leader levels, and include concrete actions and expected outcomes, including metrics that reflect not only demographic changes but also investments, vendor selection, pay equity, and other indicators of commitment (Center for Creative Leadership, 2022b).

An organization's focus, energy, and drive to create a more equitable, diverse, and inclusive culture sets the context for how much digital transformation leaders can actually achieve in their own efforts to develop more equitable, diverse, and inclusive technology teams. That context sets the parameters for what is possible. Unfortunately, the level of effort required, the resulting disruption and controversy, and the uncertainty of what "works" can be significant barriers to systemic organizational change.

And yet, human-centered leadership requires that we take on this responsibility. Equitable, diverse, and inclusive teams catalyze the technical leadership required for competitive differentiation. A more inclusive approach to recruitment will help fill the looming technology skill gap and result in well-established, positive business outcomes: all part of the financial value equation. Focusing on EDI also creates human value as we afford opportunities to participate in the creation and distribution of wealth, data representation, and AI algorithms, and inclusive participation by those being impacted by technology.

A focus on EDI as part of human-centered leadership also links to a loftier mission: Contributing to the UN Sustainable Development Goals. Six of the UN Sustainability Goals relate to the intersection of leadership, EDI, and technology. It's worth reviewing these goals because they can help connect organizations' DEI commitments to the greater good and because they identify opportunities for specific organizational action.

Education:

- By 2030, ensure equal access for all women and men to affordable and quality technical, vocational, and tertiary education, including university.
- By 2030, substantially increase the number of youth and adults who have relevant skills, including technical and vocational skills, for employment, decent jobs, and entrepreneurship.
- By 2030, eliminate gender disparities in education and ensure equal access to all levels of education and vocational training for the vulnerable, including persons with disabilities, Indigenous peoples, and children in vulnerable situations.

Good health and well-being: Substantially increase health financing and the recruitment, development, training, and retention of the health workforce in developing countries, especially in least-developed countries and small island developing states.

Gender equality: Ensure women's full and effective participation and equal opportunities for leadership at all levels of decision-making in political, economic, and public life.

- Enhance the use of enabling technology, in particular information and communications technology, to promote the empowerment of women.

Decent work and economic growth: Achieve higher levels of economic productivity through diversification, technological upgrading, and innovation, including through a focus on high-value added and labor-intensive sectors.

Industry, innovation, infrastructure: Enhance scientific research, upgrade the technological capabilities of industrial sectors in all countries, in particular developing countries, including, by 2030, encouraging innovation and substantially increasing the number of research and development workers per million people and public and private research and development spending.

Partnerships for the goals: By 2020, enhance capacity-building support to developing countries, including least developed countries and small island developing states, to significantly increase the availability of high-quality, timely, and reliable data disaggregated by income, gender, age, race, ethnicity, migratory status, disability, geographic location, and other characteristics relevant in national contexts.

While we've laid out the financial and human value case for focusing on EDI in technology, we acknowledge the truly difficult work that lies ahead. Should the organization choose to engage, we recommend investigating various frameworks for creating systemic change (Center for Creative Leadership, 2022a) and also caution that a "check-the-box" approach will not work (Caleo & Heilman, 2019). Commitment to equity, diversity, and inclusion must be a critical, strategic component of the transformational mandate that creates both economic and social value.

Key Takeaways and Actions for Developing Equitable, Diverse, and Inclusive Technology Cultures

Creating more equitable, diverse, and inclusive technology teams affords opportunities to create competitive technical leadership and realize a substantive financial return. Commitment to EDI in digital transformation also is a human-centered leadership principle and connects to every level of leadership, from the individual leader through the societal levels. DT leaders can take personal responsibility for several actions that can lead to greater systemic change:

(1) **Change your beliefs and practices by engaging in radical reflection:** Ask provocative questions about your own beliefs. Who do you believe belongs in tech? As you lead, how do you perpetuate practices that maintain the status quo? Reflect on who is in power and why, and what policies and practices should change in order to share power more equitably.

(2) **Change your models for hiring technology talent:** Widen the funnel of who might be considered in the recruitment process by deliberately reaching out to community colleges, technology associations for women and people of color, and historically black colleges. Ensure the language used in job descriptions appeals to a diverse group of people. Be adamant about having a diverse candidate slate that includes at least "two in the pool." Finally, ensure that the interviewing process is fair and equitable with clear guidelines and criteria for interviewing and evaluating candidates.

(3) **Improve inclusion practices to offer equitable opportunities for development:** When assigning tasks, make sure that all team members have the opportunity to participate in high-profile, prestigious development projects that may result in substantial financial returns or intellectual property rights. Provide

constructive feedback to everyone; don't hold back because you have assumptions or biases about who is "sensitive." Yes, mentor, but more importantly, sponsor.

(4) Develop equitable pathways to technology careers: The looming technology worker gap will challenge DT leaders to invest in new pathways for technical talent. Developing partnerships with community colleges, trade schools, and other organizations will help fill the gap and open gateways to women and people of color entering the technology sector. These equitable pathways clearly link to the UN Sustainability Goals.

(5) Clarify how AI will be developed and governed: Machine-learning algorithms will undoubtedly be part of any digital transformation initiative. DT leaders must understand which decisions have been automated by machines and whether those machine algorithms create fair outcomes. DT leaders can stay informed on advancements in AI, learn about the various types of bias, and ask discerning questions of the development team.

We acknowledge that these steps are only the beginning. The case study we included demonstrated how small initiatives can create momentum within an organization. However, individual and team leadership must be accompanied by organizational commitment. Creating a more equitable, diverse, and inclusive technology culture must become a part of the transformation mandate, tying to corporate purpose, and be a key aspect of human-impact decision-making as organizations develop and implement technology.

Conclusion: The Human-Centered Approach to EDI

Human-centered digital transformation leadership requires our ability to create equitable, diverse, and inclusive technology cultures.

The benefits are clear: Attracting investment, improved innovation, competitive talent acquisition and retention strategies, and enhanced brand reputations. That's a compelling "doing well" story. EDI work also creates enormous opportunities to do good, from equitable participation in wealth creation to the ethical use of AI to advancing the UN sustainability goals. The work requires concerted effort from both the organization and individual DT leaders.

In the following chapter, we present a case study that illustrates how a nonprofit organization has put multiple DT leadership capabilities into action. We'll see how technology and the team culture reflect a focus on EDI but with an intriguing twist.

Chapter 8

Case Study:
Transforming Foster Care

In September of 2021, the *New York Times* published a guest essay by Sixto Cancel, the CEO of Think of Us (TOU), an organization dedicated to driving equitable systems change "so that the youth and families most impacted by foster care have the greatest power and opportunity to reshape it" (Cancel, 2021). In his remarkable essay, Mr. Cancel described the trauma he experienced as a foster child and his determination to change the broken system struggling to serve over 600,000 US children. With Mr. Cancel at the helm, TOU has become a catalyst for changing the foster care system, one that uplifts, rather than exploits, the youth and families it is meant to serve. This case study explores that journey as Mr. Cancel and the TOU team combine technology, data and analytics, partnerships, and policy advocacy to create positive outcomes with and for the people with lived experiences in the foster care system.

A Brief Look at the Foster Care System

Children enter the foster care system because of a report of neglect or abuse. With the approval of a judge, the local Department of Social Services can take custody of a child(ren) and place the child(ren) in alternative living arrangements including group homes, foster placements, or with kin. These custodial arrangements are *intended* to be temporary. Ideally, children will be reunited with their parent(s) after the parent(s) demonstrate they can care for their children, a standard that includes stable housing and a source of income. If parent(s) cannot show they can adequately care for their child(ren), then adoption is usually pursued, ideally with kin (grandparents, siblings, aunts, uncles, etc.). This sounds like a reasonable process to protect at-risk children: (1) provide children with foster parents who can provide adequate resources and supervision, (2) assist parent(s) so they can stabilize and be equipped to care for their children, (3) prioritize placing children back with their parents/families, and (4) if this is not possible, place children with kin or in an adoptive home. Millions of well-meaning people — foster care families, social workers, health care workers, lawyers, judges, volunteers, and federal and state policymakers — work within this system to achieve positive outcomes for the children in their care.

Inside the system, parents must demonstrate to a judge that they can care for their child(ren). Custody will then be transferred from social services back to the parents. This process involves creating parent case plans with specific steps for achieving reunification, supervision of foster parents and the children in their care, separate legal representation of the parents, the children, and social services, and specific plans to meet the foster child's physical health, mental health, and education needs. The costs of this system are enormous, consuming about $5.3 billion annually of federal government spending. Ironically, only about $559 million is spent on prevention and permanence services. In other words, the federal government spends almost ten times more on foster care and adoption than on programs geared toward reunification (Brico, 2019). In this case study, we'll look at how TOU is working to change those outcomes using data and digital technologies. The systemic approach has implications for all levels of leadership and offers unique perspectives on developing inclusive cultures and psychological safety.

Instruments of Change: The Digital Journey

From the beginning, Mr. Cancel envisioned that digital technologies could help transform the child welfare system: By collecting data about what foster youth actually need and developing case management software, Think of Us could both lower costs and provide the insights needed to drive policy change. In the early days, TOU was focused on building an app to support older youth transitioning out of the foster care system. TOU chose to prototype and test a range of services to support these youth including a digital locker for their critical documents, which are often lost during the frequent moves or not available without requesting confidential case files. Meanwhile, TOU also hosted hackathon events to gather ideas for technology products that would revolutionize supervised visitations between parents and their children. This exploratory process highlighted the need to digitally transform the case management software used in many foster care systems.

When children are placed into foster care, parents may or may not have the right to visit their children. For some families, visitation is allowed but must be supervised by a caseworker in a setting provided by child services. States coordinate these visits and the information collected about the visit in one of two ways: A cumbersome manual process of emails and phone calls or the use of case management software. The manual process is extremely inefficient, and case management software from technology platform providers can be very expensive.

In addition, the logistics of coordinating supervised visits are complex and have ramifications for the parents and their children living in foster care. These supervised visitations involve the parent(s), the child in foster care, a caseworker, frequently a *guardian ad litem*, and the coordination of transportation by the foster parents or others. Often, parents must confirm their visit 24 hours before the visit, and if they do not, the visit is canceled. In addition, caseworkers must compile notes about the visit that are later used in court reports. The arcane manual system of phone calls and emails creates enormous inefficiencies. Worse, miscommunications on the timing and confirmation of supervised visits can cost parents and children the opportunity to see one another.

As time moved forward, the vision — and the opportunity connected with it — began to expand. In 2019, TOU received funding from the New Profit Accelerator Initiative. The selection of this partner was very deliberate. New Profit supports social entrepreneurs who "center equity in their work and who are proximate to the communities we collectively aim to serve." New Profit's philosophy matched perfectly with Mr. Cancel's commitment that the people with lived experience in the foster care system lead TOU. Funds from New Profit allowed TOU to begin experimenting with how to expand from digital technologies to driving systemic change.

A second funding opportunity emerged as states began examining the costs of foster care case management software. State Child Services organizations around the country spend millions of dollars on case management software. These case management software applications have a variety of features to organize information so those involved in the care of the child can coordinate information and resources, including managing supervised visits. But the costs are high and the features for managing supervised visits can miss the mark. When an opportunity to solve this problem emerged, the TOU team used it as a way to experiment with digital technology using a collaborative approach.

The Department of Child Services in Los Angeles, California, estimated spending 2 million hours a year arranging 4 million hours of foster child visits. To address the problem, the department applied for and received a grant to prototype a technology application. They chose to partner with Sidebench, an app developer, to build the prototype. The collaboration resulted in a new minimum viable product, where the new tool acted as a "filing cabinet where all visits and visit requests are attached to the case in question and organized around the request itself."

As the team innovated, they learned some hard lessons, not the least of which were the barriers to implementing a new software given embedded case management systems. The team also came to change their position on the ultimate goals for case management systems: Data collected by the software could provide new insights into how to create positive outcomes. The team envisioned that the software could identify resources and pathways that would help families stay together. In 2020, experiments with the case management prototype were underway, and then the global pandemic upended everything. A new and urgent opportunity emerged for digital technology to transform the system.

The Global Pandemic: A Swift Data-Driven Response

The COVID-19 crisis provided an unprecedented opportunity for TOU to demonstrate how digital transformation, data, and partnerships could drive positive outcomes for foster youth. During the pandemic, TOU leveraged data it collected about the experiences and needs of 27,000 youth who were aging out of the foster care system. TOU used the data to advocate Congress allocating funds to help youth in need. The result? $400 million in state funding for COVID relief for foster youth. TOU then shared data with states so they understood the needs of youth in their jurisdiction and could allocate funds. States could use the monies to cover expenses like rent, groceries, transportation, education, and utilities. While this was a great start, TOU recognized that getting these monies to youth in desperate need would be nearly impossible: No national, and in most cases, statewide databases of former foster youth existed. The relief program timeframe was extremely short — monies would only be available from March to September 2021. However, states did not have the infrastructure or staffing to market, process applications, and rapidly disperse funding for the program. Each state was left to its own devices for developing a distribution plan, including eligibility, payment amount, notification for eligible applicants, monitoring restrictions on the use of funds, and actually disbursing the funds (Wasch, 2021). State commissioners needed to write a memo with a plan for how monies would be used. As states wrestled with these issues, the money sat and days ticked by. Meanwhile, foster youth faced the pandemic without support for food, housing, and education.

TOU mobilized a remarkable response that leveraged technology, data, and an ecosystem of partnerships. They first addressed finding the foster youth in need of help given the lack of a centralized database. They began collecting information from former foster youth across the country who wanted to apply for COVID relief, partnering with over 200 youth-serving and BIPOC organizations to find current and former foster youth. This resulted in over 33,000 foster youth who responded with information and requests for help. The TOU team then needed to connect states to youth in need and create a system to rapidly process applications for assistance. The team built a custom application portal, ultimately used by 24 states, that included customized templates for each state to create the required memos to obtain the federal funding and connect with youth. National town halls were held with youth to understand their most critical needs for funding. In turn, these needs were communicated to the states to ensure funds were actually allocated. The outcomes? Thirty states joined a community of practice to receive support in finding and connecting with eligible young people (including marketing and social media assets designed by individuals with lived experience). Over 30,000 youth connected with their states and were able to receive these critical funds. In addition, TOU extended the lessons learned by publishing an implementation report with the Youth Law Center to inform White House and Congressional strategy based on direct feedback from the 30 states.

The TOU team encountered barrier after barrier during this process. They needed to build a data collection portal with young people that provided a user-friendly interface. They needed to address data privacy and security issues as personally identifiable information data needed to be shared in order to allocate funds. They needed to verify applications and find ways to get funds to approved youth in need. They needed to design and collect the right information to understand the current conditions foster youth were experiencing and the opportunities that existed to support them. And they needed to translate this information to influence policy change. All of this took place while TOU held true to its mandate that the people with lived experiences in the foster experience *must* be part of designing the new system.

TOU's responses reflected a culture that was digitally ready. In Chapter 5, we presented an organizational digital readiness capability model. TOU exemplified many of these capabilities. Everyone understood the transformation mandate: Create pathways to disperse $400 million in COVID relief to foster youth in need. TOU focused on *customer centricity* by creating solutions for two customers: foster youth who had aged out of the system and the states whose hands were tied because they had no contact information. The organization demonstrated *organizational agility* by deftly taking a needs-based approach and thoughtfully considering how to best mobilize states through *operational excellence*. At every step of the way, they focused on *collaboration* as they mobilized over 200 partners to find and connect youth to funding. They were *resilient* in overcoming barriers big and small. And, they have now leveraged this foundational work into new opportunities for applying digital technologies.

The Center for Lived Experience

The determined work of TOU and their partners resulted in a new data asset: Between their initial MicroCash Grant survey and the Check for Us campaign, TOU built a database of nearly 30,000 former foster care youth who had aged out of the system: the first comprehensive dataset of its kind. The data include demographic information, primary needs, the impact of COVID-19 on respondents, financial security, food security, and housing. Information may be aggregated by demographic information, and critically, is available at the state level. The data now represent another enormous opportunity to leverage technology, partnerships, and policy change to create better outcomes for foster youth and have become the backbone of a new initiative: The Center for Lived Experience.

The Center for Lived Experience will build and collect evidence that can be used by an entire ecosystem dedicated to creating positive outcomes for foster children. The people with lived experience are at

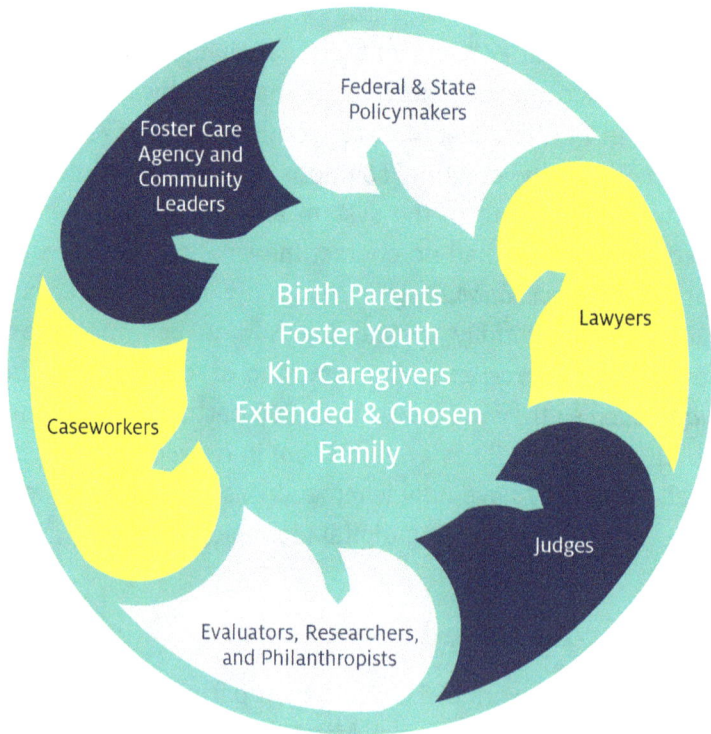

Figure 1:   Think of Us partnership ecosystem.

the center of this system. These birth parents, foster children, kin caregivers, and extended and chosen family members will direct the system to meet their needs. These needs will then inform the ecosystem of what must be done to create positive outcomes. The ecosystem itself includes policymakers, the legal system, research and evaluation, philanthropists, caseworkers, foster care agencies, and community leaders. All are invited to the table to participate and learn (Figure 1).

The Center for Lived Experience will integrate the insights, data, and leadership of people with lived experience to rearchitect the child welfare system. TOU has begun soliciting project ideas from the ecosystem on how to leverage the existing data and continue to evolve it, including creating connections with foster care youth, mobilizing communities, and creating new technologies to solve problems.

Instruments of Change: Digital Transformation Leadership

In this mission-driven, technology-enabled, and fast-moving organization, what does digital leadership look like? What is the culture that Mr. Cancel and the team are creating for themselves and their partners? We identified several digital transformation leadership capabilities discussed in Chapter 3 that exemplify the working model at TOU, beginning with *solving problems inclusively* and a *results orientation*. Mr. Cancel emphasizes that results are the first priority of the TOU culture. He noted, "Trying hard is not good enough, we have to build it right. And to do that we must be relentless about barriers and shifting around those barriers — something always comes up." TOU hires people who are both curious and persistent in getting to a result. And getting to that result has been fostered by focusing on building an equitable, diverse, and inclusive team. Mr. Cancel stated that "diversity is where things thrive" because it creates more effective problem solving. And at TOU, diversity has two meanings. Of course, people of color, men and women, LGBTQ+, and other underrepresented groups are deliberately sought and hired. However, two other views of diversity are critical: (a) political views, because of the close work with government agencies on policy change, and (b) the deliberate, intentional focus on hiring people from the foster care system. The people who are most impacted by the problem should be the people solving the problem: *Not about us without us.*

Psychological safety also plays a critical role. The combination of people's differing views allows TOU to take very different and impactful approaches to transforming foster care. Work between team members is "honest and nondirective" as the team identifies and tackles barriers to their mission. But with that comes expectations for courage in a results-oriented culture. Mr. Cancel stated, "We have no space for people who cannot bring forward what is wrong. We must have that environment. It's important to take that responsibility. I'd rather have someone consistently bringing up issues than someone who's not."

Digital leadership capabilities also show up in the keen orientation toward research as the organization continuously *evaluates the landscape* and *finds opportunities* for digital solutions. The case management software prototype, the Center for Lived Experience, and the research-backed, outcomes-based approach have both exemplified how results are transforming approaches to foster care. The team's focus on partnerships and the clear, data-driven categorization of the actual needs of foster youth have *energized ecosystems* to change how the system operates, understanding the nuance of the problems and designing effective solutions. As TOU continues to grow, digital transformation leadership will continue to be critical to achieving its mission.

The Partnership Ecosystem

TOU has always focused on a partnership ecosystem. Mr. Cancel noted that the purpose of activating this ecosystem is to create "intersections." By building an effective feedback loop, there can be "meaningful engagement points and the ability to equip people with knowledge and resources to get the work done." A second leg of the partnership ecosystem is to shape national child welfare policies, shifting the ways that laws are made, carried out, and enforced by working every step of the way with the people impacted by those laws.

The future

What TOU will look like in three to five years is changing rapidly. The organization has successfully demonstrated how research, technology, and data can mobilize slow-moving bureaucracies and create policy change. As TOU designs its three-year strategic plan, influencing policy will be a central initiative. TOU has been engaged with high-level policymakers in the presidential administrations of Barack Obama, Donald Trump, and Joseph Biden. In 2021, TOU had 26 engagements at the White House to elevate child welfare as a priority. The organization, rather than fighting to find a place at the policy-making table, is now being invited to be at that table and lead.

The new strategy will continue to adhere to the mandate that it is driven by the people with lived experience in the foster care system. For example, the Away From Home research conducted by TOU, Casey Family Programs, and the Annie E. Casey Foundation explored the lived experiences of 78 foster youth, including those in congregate care (Fatallah & Sullivan, 2021). The report resulted in concrete recommendations for policy changes to eliminate institutionalized care and instead prevent families from ever entering the foster care system.

Data and technology will continue to be central to the strategy. The Center for Lived Experience will continue to expand as it builds the data-driven ecosystem that connects families to resources and creates the proximal policies to drive change. TOU continues to capitalize on the COVID-19 crisis center it deployed in 2020 by prototyping Virtual Support Services (VSS) centers. This digital wrap-around model gives young people and families direct access to resources, allowing users to search and apply for those resources supported by a team of locally based community responders. The holistic approach includes interactive videos, technology, a resource library, a virtual community, and live support. TOU also envisions partnering with tech companies in a Digital Collaborative to design, test, and deliver services directly to state foster care programs and solve systemic breakdowns like redistributing overstocked medication, building access to credit, distributing food stamps, career support, support for first-generation college students, and connecting to mental health support groups.

The tangled web of foster care, intended to protect children, too often has the opposite result. Mr. Cancel and the TOU team are determined to change that system through technology, data, research, community collaboration, and policy advocacy. Leading this transformational change are the people with lived experiences who can best guide the many organizations, philanthropists, and individuals who want to do good but must do so by focusing on the right outcomes. With this human-centered approach, the organization can do well by obtaining the funding needed to do good. The sky seems to be the limit. When we last spoke with Mr. Cancel, he was off to speak with the president of the United States.

Chapter 9

Case Study: A New Vision of Sustainable Mining

Sustainable mining? Mining that improves people's lives with technology and digitization? Sustainable mining may seem like an oxymoron, but the words embody the transformation this leading global mining company has mandated. In this case study, we'll refer to the company as MCo. MCo exemplifies responsible digital transformation through human-centered leadership in their efforts to develop mines that are integrated, automated, carbon neutral, use far less water, and are mindful of the communities they serve. MCo recognizes that the dual responsibilities of broad transformation through digital enablement can be realized by developing leaders with the right mindset and behaviors to execute "doing well and doing good."

The Demand for Change

Mining involves the extraction of minerals and materials from the earth, with considerable equipment, labor, and energy required to support these efforts. Beyond extraction, the mine-to-market process involves management of complex, sophisticated supply chains that are typically subject to disruption. Communities where mining takes place experience both benefits in terms of employment and mineral rights *and* the toxic environments that impact the health and socioeconomic status of those communities. This polarity will grow increasingly important to manage because demand for minerals will continue to grow as global populations grow. Infrastructure needed to serve demands for reliable power, transportation, housing, clean water, and sanitation will increase the need for minerals (Society for Mining, Metallurgy & Exploration, 2021). In addition, the World Bank estimates that over 3 billion tons of minerals and metals will be needed to deploy wind, solar, and geothermal power (Hund, La Porta, Fabregas, Laing, & Drexhage, 2020). Recycling will only be able to meet a portion of this demand. Thus, it will be necessary to continue to produce minerals from new and existing mining operations indefinitely (Mining and Metallurgical Society of America, 2021). Given this demand, it is no wonder that scientists are exploring possibilities to mine near-earth asteroids for minerals such as iron, nickel, and cobalt. In sum, mining demand will increase and has the potential to provide significant economic benefits to communities.

On the other hand, mining can create a negative social and environmental impact both while in operation and after closing. Worker safety is a critical concern. Moreover, poorly regulated mining, especially in developing economies, can frequently contribute to local human rights violations and resource conflicts. Entire environments and ecosystems can be disrupted with toxic environments left behind. In addition, the wealth created by mining is not equitably shared with the communities disrupted by mining.

New approaches to mining are required as the industry balances meeting the demands for mining and mitigating the negative impacts of mining. The competing needs represent a significant disruption to the mining industry. The industry must strengthen its role and reputation in a rapidly changing global economy by focusing on modernization, digitization, stakeholder engagement, and transparency to support a sustainable future. Some key drivers of change include (Maennling & Toledano, 2019):

- The transition to a low-carbon economy (low-emission energy and transportation systems are more mineral-intensive and costly than their fossil fuel-based counterparts) has created more scrutiny of ESG goals and compliance. While demand for green metals and minerals increases, mining companies must reduce their own emissions and ensure that supply chains are both transparent and green.
- The increasing geopolitics of mining, global trade, and economic protectionism means that global commodity demand has become unstable; supply chains have experienced severe disruptions.
- As the world's reserves are depleted and extraction costs rise, companies must develop new technologies for extraction and improve digitization for more targeted and efficient mining.
- The notion of a social contract for mining, or license to operate, is a prerequisite for continued business. Creating benefits for local mining communities and finding alternative employment for jobs that are replaced by automation has become critical to reduce local opposition to mining.
- Modern mining workforces are evolving to support all the changes mentioned above. From a focus on remote work to critical IT skills to stakeholder engagement, the speed at which mining companies will be able to roll out new technologies at their mining sites will be closely linked to the host government's and labor unions' acceptance of reduced employment and procurement opportunities.
- Closely linked to this is the need for big data skills and data transparency not only to optimize operations but also for value

chain transparency, access to sustainability-focused investors and buyers, and disclosure to communities.

These advances are typical of an industry in transition. The drivers of change alter both market demand and the types of jobs required. More importantly, for human-centered leadership, they place completely different requirements on how leaders prepare mining organizations to succeed in the future.

The Leadership Response by MCo

MCo's purpose and strategy have evolved to address the industry challenges described above. Driving innovations that can create better outcomes for all stakeholders through a combination of technology, digital transformation, and sustainability practices has become a core value and the target of significant capital investments. The innovations create financial value with more competitive operations and production of future-enabling metals and minerals while creating human value by working toward a cleaner, greener, more sustainable world and enabling better lives for all its stakeholders. The orientation toward sustainability must apply to all activities in MCo's mining value chain, from exploration to planning, building, mining, processing, moving, and marketing to customers.

In practice, what might this look like? How are leaders expected to work and think differently? MCo leaders are constantly developing and implementing step-change innovations that are transforming mining and ensuring that communities and stakeholders benefit at the same time. Examples include underground transportation tunnels that minimize environmental impact, zero-emission hydrogen-powered haul trucks, remote operating centers that promote employee safety and well-being through reduced on-site work, best-in-class responses to the COVID-19 pandemic, and conversion of used mine water to potable-quality water through reverse osmosis.

All are ambitious projects that reflect the innovation and ingenuity of MCo leaders.

The ask of MCo's leaders is to shift from a world of predictability to one of constant adaptation: leaders who can deal with constant ambiguity and cut through the noise to create a way forward while looking at the world through multiple stakeholder perspectives. This reads like a wish list of leader development, and such leadership shifts do not occur overnight. MCo understands that in order to build a community of human-centered leaders — from the *C*-suite to individual contributors — will fundamentally stretch its leaders and make them uncomfortable with their current practices. To create the human-centered digital transformation leadership required for the next 30 to 50 years, MCo invested in development initiatives that span multiple levels of leadership and collectively aim to create a digitally ready organization that balances doing well and doing good. The development programs rested on the concept of vertical development: a shift in thinking that would help the organization move away from the known practices of mining to a new future.

We introduced the concept of vertical development in Chapter 3 as a foundational component of building one's digital leadership capabilities. To review, people engaging in vertical development need to develop more complex problem-solving skills and learn to work more interdependently. The vertical development model proposes that in a complex and adaptive world, leaders must solve problems through an interdependent, collaborative mindset, developing capabilities that include strategic thinking, leading change, conflict management, and leading across boundaries (Rooke & Torbert, 2005). The opportunity to develop leaders' complex problem-solving skills, such as those required in the digital transformation of mining, depends on the presence of three conditions, all of which represent the keen focus on interdependency and collaboration (see Figure 1). Vertical development became a key component of MCo's digital leadership readiness program.

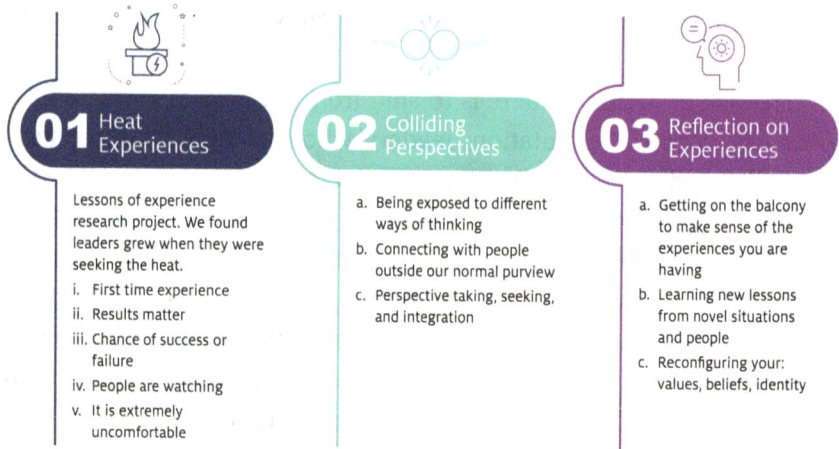

01 Heat Experiences

Lessons of experience research project. We found leaders grew when they were seeking the heat.

i.   First time experience
ii. Results matter
iii. Chance of success or failure
iv. People are watching
v.   It is extremely uncomfortable

02 Colliding Perspectives

a. Being exposed to different ways of thinking
b. Connecting with people outside our normal purview
c. Perspective taking, seeking, and integration

03 Reflection on Experiences

a. Getting on the balcony to make sense of the experiences you are having
b. Learning new lessons from novel situations and people
c. Reconfiguring your: values, beliefs, identity

Figure 1:   Catalysts for vertical development.

The Application

MCo asked CCL to collaborate with them to develop the digital transformation leaders who would lead MCo into the sustainable future it envisioned. MCo recognized that while developing the individual leaders of the future, they must also change the organizational culture. To do this, they needed to address two conditions for leadership development:

1. To focus on simultaneous development of horizontal skills and vertical leadership practices. Horizontal development requires that leaders be exposed to the individual digital leadership capabilities described in Chapter 3. Vertical development requires the introduction of transformational thinking and behaviors, enabling leaders to embrace a more complex, systemwide orientation toward *sustainable* mining that improves people's lives with technology and digitization.
2. To develop leaders at different levels within MCo simultaneously. Based on the principles outlined in Chapter 5, creating

organizational readiness requires an interdependent approach to enable the organization to receive newly developed leaders with openness, and to be psychologically and behaviorally resilient.

In this chapter, we focus on condition (1) above. We describe one of several leader levels, as an example of digital leadership development. Condition (2) was a more extensive effort over three years to interpret the same horizontal and vertical development themes at different levels of complexity and to create interdependence between the leader levels through deep commitment to cross-boundary practices: mentoring and sponsorship, innovation and experimentation, storytelling, purposeful development of networks, focus on high performing teams, boundary spanning leadership, and ecosystem engagement.

We have chosen to describe the journey of midlevel managers and professionals who would become MCo's future functional and operational leaders. Many digital leadership development efforts focus on senior leaders. MCo wanted to develop the same capabilities at lower levels and at scale. Individual leaders had to be equipped to respond skillfully to the uncertainty and changes described in this chapter, and to learn introductory methods to create a better, more sustainable future for mining, for all stakeholders and communities. This entailed thinking deeply about sustainability, including environment, social and governance implications, and an orientation toward using innovation and digital transformation to find solutions to improve lives. Importantly, it needed to be done in a safe manner that emphasized exploration and learning over achievement. Psychological safety was key. The resulting learning journey blended building individual digital leadership capabilities with learning methods that would create the interdependent, collaborative leadership required to solve the increasingly complex problems of sustainable mining. Table 1 illustrates the objectives and learning methods of this journey.

Table 1: Integration of vertical and horizontal development capabilities and learning methods

Digital Transformation Leadership Program

MINDSET SHIFT	LEADERSHIP CAPABILITIES	OBJECTIVES	KEY LEARNING METHODS
Understand the landscape: *Understand industry drivers and stakeholder value creation.*	• Future of mining and strategic opportunities • Assess digital capacity • Create psychological safety	• Develop insights into future of mining and strategic implications • Understand impact of MCo on stakeholder communities • Develop understanding of 'value' based on doing well and doing good for human-impact decision-making • Apply current MCo transformation initiatives to role and purpose	• Facilitated workshops • Exposure to digitally transformed and sustainable mining initiatives • Global virtual immersions • Simulations • Group innovation projects
Translate the possibilities: *Diagnose and improve systems, processes and services*	• Embrace calculated risk • Solve problems inclusively • Leverage data for decisions • Create psychological safety	• Experiment with new ideas and prototypes • Enhance stakeholder collaboration to support decision-making • Apply data analytics to innovation projects • Develop business communication and data visualization skills	• Teams assigned to innovation projects prioritized by MCo • Data-driving decision-making embedded in design thinking and innovation practices
Realize transformation: *Development of resilience, self-awareness, and collaboration capabilities*	• Energize ecosystems • Empower teams • Be resilient in change • Transform yourself • Create psychological safety	• Develop self-awareness and personal leadership capabilities • Increase commitment to safety leadership and psychological safety to ensure employee well-being • Build external and internal networks (across commodities, functions, and geographies) to drive collaboration • Cultivate positive team management practices • Build cultural intelligence capability to support MCo's inclusion and diversity policy	• Identify key leadership challenges • Personal data: 360 surveys, digital leadership surveys, leader network diagnostics, pulse surveys to gather feedback • 1-1 coaching • Team feedback through the innovation process • Global networking events • AI-driven learning assistant

The program structure to address these challenges integrated the three primary conditions for vertical leader development — heat experiences, colliding perspectives, and reflection — with content learning. Heat experiences were created through global, immersive experiences and team innovation work. Interaction with challenging and diverse thought leaders and extensive interaction with internal and external networks became a crucible for colliding perspectives. Coaching, feedback, and reflection enabled personal transformation to support external learning. Throughout, the journey emphasized sustainability and working with the polarities described in Chapter 4, creating an experience that encourages participants to consider the far-reaching implications and potential contradictions of digital transformation.

From Design to Implementation: Lessons Learned

Being aware of the need for a systemic shift, MCo knew that digital leadership could not be learned in isolation. The dedication and focus required of individual leaders extended to all of MCo's supporting structures. Learners operated in teams, complemented by learning support from leaders inside and outside MCo, exposing them to new points of view and broadening their thinking (colliding perspectives). Business leaders at all levels provided content, mentored groups, gave talks, hosted virtual immersions, and committed to generating excitement around digital innovations and sponsored innovation groups. Each year, an average of 45 of MCo's senior leaders were closely involved. This level of commitment and engagement from the organization and senior leadership has energized participants and highlighted the importance of the program and the transformational mandate to shift to sustainable mining.

Digital leadership cannot be learned overnight. MCo committed to "doing it properly" which meant investment in longer learning journeys. Lengthy journeys can be particularly challenging for participants, and that was true for the leaders at MCo. At times participants could become discouraged, particularly with an innovation process (a heat experience) that requires a mindset shift. This shift in mindset — asking people to "think differently" — required that they embrace nonlinear approaches. This meant understanding problems before jumping to solutions, iterating, learning to fail forward, to pivot, and to make decisions to "learn" rather than to "achieve" results, and to trust the process. Stretch and discomfort was evident.

"Mindset shift" looks different in every organization and is not an end game. When developing digital leaders, most clients articulate "mindset shift" as an outcome or end goal. Mindset shift needs to be well understood, and it will not happen in a vacuum. For MCo, most of the program participants were engineers and operations specialists with formidable analytical and technical skills. A midpoint survey showed the very things that made them good in their roles made them uncomfortable with innovation leadership, including experimentation and learning from failure. They feared they would be penalized if they didn't exhibit brilliant, predictable results at all times. Similarly, the nature of their daily work focused on stability and predictability to a large extent, all factors that support earlier stages of vertical development and not the later-stage approaches required for complex thinking and transformative change. Linked to these shifts are the capabilities to overcome fear of failure, to support experimentation and agility, to take risks, and to build psychologically safe environments for team collaboration.

MCo was careful to acknowledge these fears and promote a psychologically safe environment for learning. For example, as teams tackled innovation projects, senior leaders stressed that the teams' work would not be viewed as a "test" of their capabilities and the business value of proposed innovation projects. *How* they addressed issues and *what* they learned as they worked together as a team was more important. But this psychologically safe environment could not occur without a direct intervention that clarified the program goals: the demonstration of good leadership rather than the invention of a good product. With that clarification, real learning started to emerge: the type of learning that supports digital transformation. Uncovering this issue was critical to the success of the program. It illustrated that mindset shift does not happen without psychological safety and that leadership will not change or develop unless the context in which it operates changes at the same time.

Has the program accomplished its goals? Short and longer-term post-program surveys measured the perspectives of participants on how their leadership capabilities have been impacted by the program. Some of the findings include the following:

- An estimated **66%** improvement was seen in team engagement.
- Significant improvements in the team's psychological safety, innovation and experimentation, full-impact decision-making (i.e., balanced decision-making to enable sustainability), and stakeholder satisfaction were observed.
- **93%** of participants reported their preparedness for future leadership responsibilities had improved.
- **90%** of participants reported they have improved actively considering diverse stakeholders in decision-making.
- **90%** of participants felt they had improved in demonstrating inclusive leadership behaviors.

These results indicate a shift in both horizontal leadership capabilities and vertical development practices. Individual leaders themselves felt they had transformed and were more able to achieve the goals of the organization. Sustaining this learning is key. At the time of writing this chapter, the design team was implementing digital nudging to support the learning post-program to sustain these changes.

Summary

Digital leadership is a complex construct and requires careful development. It challenges general models of leadership because of the responsibilities for complex problem-solving that combines the creation of financial value with optimizing the impact on humanity. Just as we ask those who engage and transform as digital transformation leaders, learning and development practitioners must test and refine new approaches and methodologies to developing human-centered leadership approaches. Practitioners must take the risk of engaging in new partnerships and building approaches from scratch as we co-learn with our leader-clients on how we create a sustainable world.

Chapter 10

Our Responsibility to the World

Introduction

Klaus Schwab, founder and executive chairman of the World Economic Forum, coined the term *Fourth Industrial Revolution* in 2016. Previous industrial revolutions focused on automation, liberating humankind from animal power, creating factories for mass production, and bringing the possibilities of digital technologies to billions of people. In his book *The Fourth Industrial Revolution*, Schwab describes a world that encompasses diverse fields from material science to nanotechnology, energy, and biology, supported by a range of new technologies that are "fusing the physical, digital and biological worlds, impacting all disciplines, economies and industries, and even challenging ideas about what it means to be human" (Schwab, 2017). These new technological wonders have the potential to create a better future for humanity. However, Schwab also issued a stern warning that without deliberate collaboration across geographies, industry sectors, and research disciplines, societies will become increasingly fragmented and the socioeconomic chasm will become insurmountable.

DT leaders must heed Schwab's warning as the new Fifth Industrial Revolution gains momentum. Industry 5.0 envisions that technology and innovation best practices are directed toward the service of humanity, answering Schwab's warning and call to action

(Nahavandi, 2019). This view of industrial revolution recognizes the interdependence between human and machine using cognitive computing and human intelligence, driven by mass customization and personalization for humans. In this scenario, technology trends turn from a focus on the next new technology to how technology may support humanity. It envisions a world of deep, multilevel cooperation between humans and machines, not the replacement of humans by machines. It is an inspiring and aspirational vision of our digital future.

Digital transformation leaders have the sobering obligation to achieve the vision of Industry 5.0: We must take responsibility for ensuring that technology benefits rather than exploits humans. This weighty responsibility merits our investment. Human-centered leadership is urgently needed. Even as we write this book, debates rage over the threats to humanity posed by generative AI, the governance of social media platforms and free speech, neurotechnology that can change behavior and thought patterns ..., the list is seemingly endless. Unfortunately, our current DT leadership frameworks do not account for the need to create both economic and social values. Instead, the frameworks continue to focus on the what and how of digital transformation rather than the why.

The literature on digital transformation includes several models that outline the steps to be followed in formulating and executing a digital transformation strategy (see Bellantuono, Nuzzi, Pontrandolfo, Scozzi, 2021, for a review of these models). In Table 1, we have consolidated these models to illuminate the current thinking about digital transformation, albeit without specific attention to adopting a human-centered approach.

In the majority of DT efforts, organizations focus on understanding the competitive and financial advantages of digitization. The broader, human-centered impacts are often not discussed or are considered tangential. Business objectives continue to dominate the conversation, focusing on size, cost, and timing of returns on the DT effort. The organization pays attention to leadership alignment and

Table 1:   Existing digital transformation models

Phase	Activities	Tools/Methods
Clarifying Benefits	• Assess what's working/what's not • Understand what digitization can do • Assess current state of digital maturity • Identify gaps between what is and what is possible/best practices • Understand transformation costs/benefits/risks • Build commitment at the top	• Stakeholder input • SWOT • Financial analysis • Benchmarking • Use cases • Expert input
Setting Direction	• Set long-term vision and objectives for DT • Determine strategic positioning of the firm • Define desired digital business model • Prioritize opportunities/targets/scope	• Business model design • Balanced scorecard • Define success
Preparing for Transformation	• Digital education/upskilling • Assess organizational readiness for change • Appoint transformation team/task force • Digital education/upskilling • Assess organizational readiness for change • Appoint transformation team/task force • Employee engagement/communications	• Readiness assessment • Talent analysis/acquisition/development • Engagement labs
Needs Analysis	• Process mapping • Customer experience • Value creation network • Data management enrichment	• As is versus desired process map for each unit/function • Customer journey map • Value chain analysis

(Continued)

Table 1:   (*Continued*)

Phase	Activities	Tools/Methods
DT Roadmap	• Application of digital technologies • Design customer experience • Organization redesign • Leadership development • Culture change • Change management • Digital risk management • Resource allocation • Talent strategy for digital upskilling • Partner integration • Transformation dashboard	• Roadmap to implement new digital profile • Project management • Control tower • Ecosystem mapping • Project portfolio
Piloting	• Prioritize projects • Agile testing	• Pareto analysis against criteria for project impact/lighthouse projects • Agile methodologies • Create digital factories/proof of concept
Scaling	• Diffuse perfected approaches	• Appoint power users
Monitoring	• Process monitoring	• Balanced scorecard • Cross-functional after-action reviews
Adapting	• Continuous improvement	• Kaizen

change leadership only to the extent that these human-centered approaches can achieve the desired outcomes as quickly and profitably as possible. Very few of these efforts include the question, "I wonder how digitization might allow us to improve our culture and our positive impact on the world?" Even with the increased scrutiny of how organizations will deliver against ESG goals, or the call from employees to clarify and adhere to corporate purpose, the focus of digital transformation still tends to be about creating financial value without considering human value. This model of DT leadership can no longer serve us as we face the profound uncertainties of technological change.

We are certainly not apologists when it comes to advances in technology and their sometimes disruptive impact on our lives or the planet. We understand that technological advances can have enormous benefits for both. We understand that competitive pressures make time-to-market a critical consideration, and slowing down to consider the human impact may create some missed opportunities. However, we argue that human-centered issues, values, and ethics must be given focused attention as we develop and implement new technologies. This discipline must become as embedded in digital transformation processes as the detailed plans for adoption and scaling.

In this book, we have framed digital transformation leadership as taking place across an entire organization at three levels: The senior leadership group, the interdependent formal and informal teams that represent the interconnected organization, and the broader stakeholder ecosystem. Each group has a particular responsibility for creating both financial and human values:

- The senior leadership group must establish a transformation mandate that explains the "why" behind digital transformation and connects that why to both corporate purpose and the ongoing digital sensing that centers DT in the strategic process. This group must have direction, alignment, and commitment (DAC) before the organization can move forward.
- Individual leaders, formal and informal teams, and the organization share ownership in the processes of internal execution and scaling. We introduced two new DT leadership capability models that help the organization achieve both the interdependent work and organizational resilience to be digitally ready.

- Finally, we developed a view of a stakeholder ecosystem that governs balanced investments to achieve both financial value and broader ESG goals and human value. The stakeholder community owns responsibility for human-impact decision-making.

Our model of DT transformation leadership is intentionally different from the one described in Table 1. In contrast, our model views digital transformation as an ongoing process of strategic renewal created through human-centered leadership that results in both economic and social value. Leaders deliberately consider the human impact and seek to mitigate harm and amplify the benefits of digital technologies.

We have discussed a number of foundational concepts for human-centered leadership, organizing them by leadership level. There is much to consider in this systemic approach. In the following, we summarize some of the foundational concepts into a roadmap for change: How to begin, how to implement, and how to adapt.

How to begin: Beginnings are tremendously important. Beginnings set the stage for what is to follow. The conversations that leaders and organizations have at the beginning of digital transformation will set the course for how digital transformation proceeds, who will be included in the dialogue and decisions, and the expected outcomes. Discourse shapes reality: What we speak about to one another is what shapes planning and precedes action. What we leave out falls to the wayside. In the beginning, then, we ask that leaders pause to think about the definition of human-centered leadership:

Human-centered digital transformation leadership balances the creation of organizational financial value with the human impact on all stakeholders who create, use, or are economically, psychologically, physically, ecologically, or legally advantaged or disadvantaged by digital technologies.

Legitimizing discourse concerning the broadest impacts of DT and even formalizing an agenda that includes these topics sets the tone for what is to follow. Every discussion cannot be focused solely on time, costs, and competitive advantage. Human impact must be a focus as well. Organizations cannot hope to achieve both financial and human value goals for digital transformation if they are not made a part of the agenda from the beginning. Leaders can and must have transparent discussions and ask provocative questions: Who will participate in creating the technology? Who will benefit from the profits? Who is represented in the data? Do the benefits of the new technology clearly outweigh the potential negative consequences?

Asking and answering these questions require the perspectives of internal and external stakeholders *at the beginning.* These stakeholders can provide a wealth of insights and raise legitimate concerns about the impact of digital technologies. The release of Microsoft's new Bing chatbot illustrates how dialogue at the beginning would have prevented unwelcome controversy over the new AI technology. Satya Nadella, Microsoft's CEO, said that releasing the tool was a critical example of Microsoft's "frantic pace" to incorporate generative AI into its products (Weise & Metz, 2023). His remarks highlighted how Microsoft emphasized time-to-market over potential negative consequences. However, users quickly found that the chatbot had a troubling, even creepy, dark side. The ensuing controversy caused Microsoft to shift its frantic pace from time-to-market to damage control as they attempted to control the AI. The controversy could have been mitigated if Microsoft had involved a broader group of stakeholders from the beginning to determine how the AI would be used.

As leaders bring stakeholders into the conversation, they will be challenged to listen and think in new ways. Our model for human-centered leadership incorporates the idea of vertical development where consideration of longer-term and broader consequences is embedded in leadership development. Mary Barra, CEO of General Motors, displayed a vertical development mindset when she shifted her focus from GM's quarterly profits to setting a new vision for the future impact of the company: zero collisions, zero emissions, and zero congestion. This new mission has the potential to make GM enormously profitable and aspires to improve safety, ecological impact, and stress. Adopting human-centered leadership at the beginning of digital transformation allows leaders to set a mandate and rationale that explains to everyone why it is worthwhile and how it will benefit them. Thinking through these issues can produce another crucial benefit: creating DAC among leaders who must commit to the decision to undertake DT and maintain the course through the long, sometimes difficult, and always surprising twists and turns to follow.

How to undertake change: Experts in change management agree that involvement leads to commitment. While some popular models for DT acknowledge this, many view change management as being led by a small group of leaders who decide what should get done and then leave others to execute. However, stakeholders left out of the decision-making process will perceive that change is being done *to* them rather than *with* them. The result? Stakeholders feel angry, vulnerable, and powerless. Those feelings are the exact opposite of the conditions that support psychological safety, a foundational human-centered leadership requirement. Psychological safety lowers resistance to change and allows people to share freely what they observe and what they know. Time and again, we see examples of people holding back information during change which, if known, would have made the change effort much more successful.

As human-centered DT leaders actively seek input from stakeholders, they can also create an environment that leads to transparent dialogue. They can demonstrate their value of opinions and ideas that don't square with their own. They can ensure that a diverse group provides feedback to pinpoint issues, solve problems, and create a rich and open discussion. Likewise, human-centered DT leaders invest in the digital knowledge and capabilities of their leaders, workforce, and partners because when these parties are smarter about digital, they can contribute more to the conversation.

These leaders also foster collaborative work with formal and informal internal teams as well as external stakeholders. Two key aspects of interdependent collaboration are that (1) the parties engaged in interdependent collaboration engage in power-sharing and (2) leaders invest their own time and energy into collaboration rather than delegating the responsibility for collaboration to others. Leaders and organizations who believe that they and they alone should maintain the power to dictate the terms of DT soon discover that their power has real limits. Airbus ran into this very issue as it negotiated with over 17,000 suppliers for aircraft components. When Airbus tried to use contracts to enforce compliance from suppliers for aggressive timelines, it was met with stiff resistance. Indeed, the very processes it tried to mandate resulted in a snarled supply chain that wasted time and money. When Airbus adopted a new approach and invited suppliers to the table to power share in the development of a new digital supply chain platform, suppliers became more self-managing and streamlined the processes for manufacturing and distribution. Airbus might have wanted to avoid the work and costs associated with developing a digital supply chain management system, but it also needed the benefits that a new platform would provide. A focus on compliance with mandated contracts and processes without conversations with suppliers would never achieve the desired goals.

How to continue to adapt. Because DT is a process and not a project, learning and adaptation are part and parcel of success. The rapid pace of technological change will continuously disrupt digital strategies. New emerging technologies will introduce competitive advantages for both incumbents and new entrants. Leaders will turn over, and incoming leaders will bring new perspectives, experiences, and expectations. Competitors will take steps to counter the advantages gained, and regulators will demand more attention to intended and unintended impacts. These factors all illustrate why we focus on digital transformation as a process of strategic renewal. To continuously adapt and remain resilient, human-centered DT leaders must be equipped to renew their own skills and mindsets. They must be open to learning and to changing past decisions and directions. They must hold both themselves and team members accountable for achieving goals while avoiding the trap of setting inflexible goals that allow no room for adjustment. They must shift their own and team members' mindsets from expecting certainty to expecting uncertainty, and they must increase tolerance for the inevitable mistakes as people experiment with ways to cope with the unknown, ever-changing reality of digital transformation.

Doing well and doing good is a worthy challenge for DT leaders. We have powerful opportunities to influence humanity's future. In the next ten years, our world will see enormous technological leaps that we can barely fathom today. The seemingly unlimited list of technological innovations and their magnificent possibilities are limited only by humanity's ingenuity and imagination. Indeed, invention is joyful, awe-inspiring, and inevitable. However, we can also direct humanity's ingenuity and imagination toward creating a digital future that benefits Earth's global citizens and mitigates the potential harm of our inventions. We *can* create both financial and human values. We *can* do well and do good. We *can* be human-centered leaders because we are human.

Human-Centered Leadership
Concepts and Definitions

Balanced investment: A proportion of capital and profits is shared to achieve ESG goals that improve humanity's future.

Business model: The design or architecture of the value creation, delivery, and capture mechanisms of a firm.

Digital readiness: An organization's assessment of its state of preparedness for effective production, adoption, and exploitation of digital technologies. The organization is both psychologically and behaviorally prepared to take action.

Digital sensing: Investing in learning about digital innovations and seeing around corners to remain open to new and better applications of technology to solve problems and promote well-being.

Digital transformation: An ongoing process of strategic renewal that uses advances in digital technologies to build capabilities that refresh or replace an organization's business model, collaborative approach, and culture (Warner & Wager, 2019).

Digital transformation mandate: Providing a vision and rationale for digital transformation that explains why transformation is worthwhile and how it will benefit various stakeholders and ties to the ability to create both financial value and human value.

Direction, Alignment, and Commitment (DAC): Direction: Agreement in the group on overall goals; Alignment: Coordinated work within the group; Commitment: Mutual responsibility for the group.

Doing well and doing good: The desire to achieve benefits associated with the application of digital technologies to organizational process and business model improvements (doing well) while demonstrating concern for the impact of digital transformation on humanity and planet Earth (doing good).

Ecosystem management: Forming partnerships with individuals, groups, and agencies that can multiply the efforts a single organization could achieve.

EDI: Equity, diversity, and inclusion. *Equity*: Fair and contextually appropriate access to the resources required for an individual to attain their full potential (Center for Creative Leadership, 2023); *Diversity*: The presence of differences that may reflect different social identities, including race, gender, religion, sexual orientation, ethnicity, nationality, socioeconomic status, language, (dis)ability, age, religious commitment, or political perspective. *Inclusion*: Outcomes to ensure that all individuals feel welcome and participate fully in the decision-making processes and development opportunities within an organization or group (Extension Foundation Impact Collaborative, 2023).

ESG: A framework including environmental, social, and governance factors used by investors to evaluate corporate behavior and future financial performance (Li, Wang, Sueyoshi, & Wang 2021).

Financial value: Metrics for measuring the return on investments for digital transformation, such as profits, internal rate of return, net present value, and productivity.

Growth mindset: In a growth mindset, people believe that their most basic abilities can be developed through dedication and hard work — brains and talent are just the starting point. This view creates a love of learning and a resilience that is essential for great accomplishment (Dweck, 2017).

Human-centered digital transformation leadership: Human-centered digital transformation leadership balances the creation of organizational financial value with the human impact on all stakeholders who create, use, or are economically, psychologically, physically, or legally advantaged or disadvantaged by digital technologies.

Human-impact decision-making: A process in which all stakeholders have been accorded intrinsic value by decision-makers who carefully evaluate options to balance the creation of both economic and social value.

Human value: Metrics for measuring improvement to people's lives, including (a) organizational metrics, such as well-being, capability and skill improvements, inclusive cultures, and engagement, and (b) societal metrics, such as improvements in health-related outcomes, proportion of population living below the international (or national) poverty line, or proportion of youth and adults with information and communications technology (ICT) skills. The UN Sustainable Development Goals and indicators provide an excellent framework for thinking about human value.

Interdependent collaboration: Working with individuals and teams in a hypercollaborative fashion to achieve outcomes that could not be accomplished with less-than-full-hearted collaborative efforts. Engages the ecosystem of stakeholders.

Leadership: A social process that enables individuals to work together as a cohesive group to produce collective results (Drath *et al.*, 2008).

Organizational purpose: An organization's meaningful and enduring reason to exist that aligns with long-term financial performance, provides a clear context for daily decision-making, and unifies and motivates relevant stakeholders (Hurth, Ebert, & Prabhu, 2018).

Organizational resilience: The ability of an organization to anticipate, prepare for, respond to, and adapt to incremental change and sudden disruptions in order to survive and prosper.

Psychological safety: A shared belief held by members of a team that the team is safe for interpersonal risk-taking (Edmondson, 1999).

Punctuated equilibrium: Relatively long periods of stability (equilibrium periods) that are punctuated by relatively short bursts of fundamental change (Gersick, 1991).

Talent development: Strategies for filling digital skill gaps with the appropriate level of attention to bringing in new talent and developing existing talent.

Vertical development: The science of how the perspectives of individuals and groups can evolve to become progressively more elevated, complex, and integrated (Palus, McGuire, Stawiski, & Torbert, 2020).

Well-being: Perceptions of how well life is going, that life is satisfying. May include dimensions such as positive relationships, meaning or life purpose, engagement, mastery, optimism, and autonomy (Marsh, Huppert, Donald, Horwood, & Sahdra, 2020).

Appendix

Polarity Map® is a registered trademark of Barry Johnson and Polarity Partnerships, LLC. Commercial use encouraged with permission.

A copy of the full polarity map appears in the following. For more information about polarity mapping, see https://www.polarity partnerships.com/.

Polarity Map®

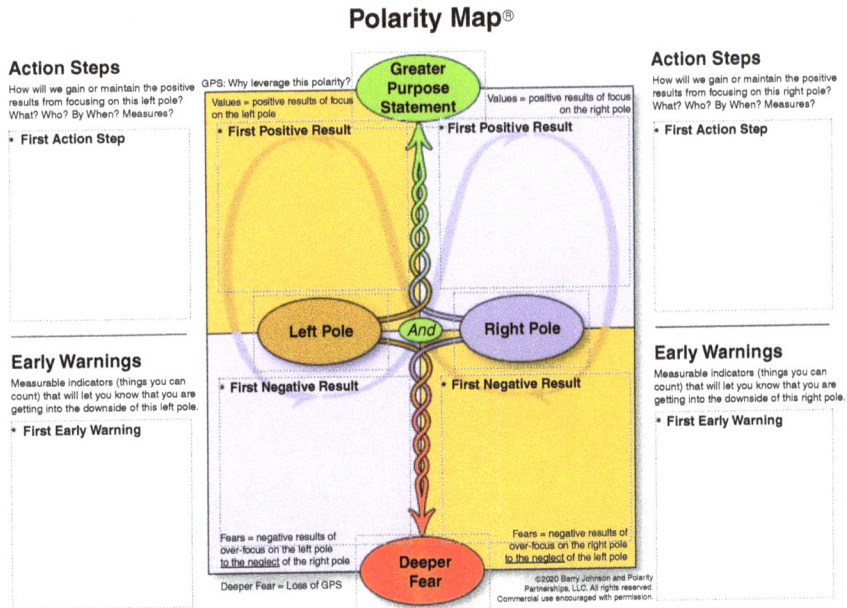

Action Steps
How will we gain or maintain the positive results from focusing on this left pole? What? Who? By When? Measures?

- First Action Step

Early Warnings
Measurable indicators (things you can count) that will let you know that you are getting into the downside of this left pole.

- First Early Warning

GPS: Why leverage this polarity?

Values = positive results of focus on the left pole

- First Positive Result

Greater Purpose Statement

Values = positive results of focus on the right pole

- First Positive Result

Action Steps
How will we gain or maintain the positive results from focusing on this right pole? What? Who? By When? Measures?

- First Action Step

Left Pole And **Right Pole**

- First Negative Result

- First Negative Result

Early Warnings
Measurable indicators (things you can count) that will let you know that you are getting into the downside of this right pole.

- First Early Warning

Fears = negative results of over-focus on the left pole to the neglect of the right pole

Deeper Fear = Loss of GPS

Fears = negative results of over-focus on the right pole to the neglect of the left pole

Deeper Fear

©2020 Barry Johnson and Polarity Partnerships, LLC. All rights reserved. Commercial use encouraged with permission.

www.PolarityPartnerships.com

191

References

Alliance, G. S. I. (2017). Global sustainable investment review 2016. http://www.gsi-alliance.org/wp-content/uploads/2021/08/GSIR-20201.pdf.

Annie E. Casey Foundation. (2020). *Annie E. Casey Foundation Kids Count Database.* https://datacenter.kidscount.org/data/tables/6242-children-0-to-17-in-foster-care.

Badall, S. B. (2014). *The business benefits of gender diversity.* Gallup. https://www.gallup.com/workplace/236543/business-benefits-gender-diversity.aspx.

Bague, H., Meaney, M., & Lund, F. (2021). *Boards, talent and culture.* McKinsey Digital. https://www.mckinsey.com/business-functions/strategy-and-corporate-finance/our-insights/boards-talent-and-culture.

Behroozi, M., Shirolkar, S., Barik, T., & Parnin, C. (2020). Does stress impact technical interview performance? *Proceedings of the 28th ACM Joint Meeting on European Software Engineering Conference and Symposium on the Foundations of Software Engineering* (pp. 481–492).

Bellantuono, N., Nuzzi, A., Pontrandolfo, P., & Scozzi, B. (2021). Digital transformation models for the I4.0 transition: Lessons from the change management literature. *Sustainability*, 13(23), 12941.

Blackman, R. (2022). *Ethical Machines: Your Concise Guide to Totally Unbiased, Transparent, and Respectful AI.* Harvard Business Review Press.

Blomstrom, D. (2021). *People Before Tech: The Importance of Psychological Safety and Teamwork in the Digital Age.* Bloomsbury Business.

Boehm, J. & Smith, J. (2021). *Derisking digital and analytics transformations.* McKinsey Digital. https://www.mckinsey.com/business-functions/risk-and-resilience/our-insights/derisking-digital-and-analytics-transformations.

Bogen, M. & Reicke, A. (2018). *An examination of hiring.* Upturn. http://hdl. voced.edu.au/10707/599715.

Brico, E. (2019). *The government spends 10 times more on foster care and adoption than reuniting families.* Talk Poverty. https://talkpoverty.org/ 2019/08/23/government-more-foster-adoption-reuniting/.

Caleo, S. & Heilman, M. E. (2019). What could go wrong? Some unintended consequences of gender bias interventions. *Archives of Scientific Psychology,* 7, 71–80.

Cancel, S. (2021, September 16). *I will never forget that I could have lived with people who loved me.* The New York Times. https://www.nytimes. com/2021/09/16/opinion/foster-care-children-us.html.

Catalyze Tech Working Group. (2021, October). *The ACT report: Action to catalyze tech, a Paradigm Shift for DEI.* Aspen Institute and Snap Inc, https://actreport.com/.

Center for an Urban Future. (2019). *Expanding tech apprenticeships in New York City.* https://nycfuture.org/pdf/CUF-ExpandingTechApprenticeships_ final_1.pdf.

Center for Creative Leadership. (2020a). *Kickstart your diversity and inclusion initiatives with a focus on equity.* https://www.ccl.org/articles/leading-effectively-articles/kick-start-your-diversity-inclusion-initiatives-with-a-focus-on-equity/.

Center for Creative Leadership. (2020b). *Talent Reimagined 2020: The human element of disruption.* https://www.ccl.org/articles/research-reports/ talent-reimagined-disruptive-trends-2020/.

Center for Creative Leadership. (2022a). *5 powerful ways to take REAL action on DEI (diversity, equity & inclusion).* https://www.ccl.org/articles/leading-effectively-articles/5-powerful-ways-to-take-real-action-on-dei-diversity-equity-inclusion/.

Center for Creative Leadership. (2022b). *Crafting meaningful corporate EDI statements.* https://www.ccl.org/wp-content/uploads/2022/06/crafting-meaningful-corporate-EDI-statements-center-for-creative-leadership-ccl.pdf.

Center for Creative Leadership. (2022c). *The 70-20-10 rule for leadership development.* https://www.ccl.org/articles/leading-effectively-articles/70-20-10-rule/.

Center for Creative Leadership. (2023). *Equity, diversity and inclusion: Moving from ideas into action.* https://www.ccl.org/leadership-challenges/equity-diversity-inclusion/.

Chang, F. (2020). *To build more-inclusive technology, change your design process.* Harvard Business Review [Internet]. https://hbr.org/2020/10/to-build-more-inclusive-technology-change-your-design-process.

Christensen, C. M. (2013). *The Innovator's Dilemma: When New Technologies Cause Great Firms to Fail.* Harvard Business Review Press.

Christensen, S. L. & Kohls, J. (2002). Ethical decision making in times of organizational crisis: A framework for analysis. *Business and Society*, 42(3), 328–358.

Chua, P. K. & Mazmanian, M. (2020). Are you one of us? Current hiring practices suggest the potential for class biases in large tech companies. *Proceedings of the 28th ACM Joint Meeting on European Software Engineering Conference and Symposium on the Foundations of Software Engineering*, 4, 481–492.

Clark, T. (2020). *The 4 Stages of Psychological Safety: Defining the Path to Inclusion and Innovation.* Berrett-Koehler.

Collier, D. & Zhang, C. (2016). *Can we reduce bias in the recruiting process and diversify pools of candidates by using different types of words in job descriptions?* Cornell University Digital Collections. https://ecommons.cornell.edu/handle/1813/74363.

Dawkins, M. & Balakrishnan, R. (2022). *Cosmetic, conversation, or commitment: A study of EDI corporate messages, motives and metrics after George Floyd's murder.* Greensboro, NC: Center for Creative Leadership.

de la Boutetiere, H., Montagner, H., & Reich, A. (2018). *Unlocking success in digital transformations.* Retrieved from McKinsey Digital, https://www.mckinsey.com/business-functions/people-and-organizational-performance/our-insights/unlocking-success-in-digital-transformations.

Dewey, J. (1929). *Experience and Nature.* W.W. Norton.

Drath, W. H., McCauley, C. D., Palus, C. J., Van Velsor, E., O'Connor, P. M., & McGuire, J. B. (2008). Direction, alignment, commitment: Toward a more integrative ontology of leadership. *Leadership Quarterly*, 19(6), 635–653.

Dweck, C. (2017). *Mindset: Changing the Way You Think to Fulfil Your Potential.* Little, Brown Book Group.

Edmondson, A. (1999). Psychological safety and learning behavior in work teams. *Administrative Science Quarterly*, 44(2), 350–383.

Extension Foundation Impact Collaborative. (2023). *Diversity, equity, and inclusion.* https://dei.extension.org/.

Fatallah, S. & Sullivan, S. (2021, July 21). *Away from home: Youth Experiences of institutional placements in foster care.* Think of Us. https://assets.website-files.com/60a6942819ce8053cefd0947/60f6b1eba474362514093f96_Away%20From%20Home%20-%20Report.pdf.

Ferdman, B. (2017). Paradoxes of inclusion: Understanding and managing the tensions of diversity and multiculturalism. *Journal of Applied Behavioral Science*, 53(2), 235–263.

Fink, L. (2022). *Larry Fink's letter to CEOs: The power of capitalism*. BlackRock. https://www.blackrock.com/corporate/investor-relations/larry-fink-ceo-letter.

Fontan, C., Alloza, A., & Rey, C. (2019). (Re)discovering organizational purpose. In C. Rey, M. Bastons, & P. Sotok (Eds.) *Purpose Driven Organizations*. Palgrave Macmillan.

Forth, P., Reichert, T., de Laubier, R., & Chakraborty, S. (2020). *Flipping the odds of digital transformation success*. Retrieved from Boston Consulting Group. https://www.bcg.com/publications/2020/increasing-odds-of-success-in-digital-transformation.

Foss, N. J. & Saebi, T. (2017). Fifteen years of research on business model innovation: How far have we come, and where should we go? *Journal of Management*, 43(1), 200–227.

Gartner. (2022). *The state of DEI*. https://www.gartner.com/en/podcasts/thinkcast/the-state-of-dei.

Gersick, C. J. (1991). Revolutionary change theories: A multilevel exploration of the punctuated equilibrium paradigm. *Academy of Management Review*, 16(1), 10–36.

Glassdoor. (2020). *Glassdoor's diversity and inclusion study*. https://www.glassdoor.com/blog/glassdoors-diversity-and-inclusion-workplace-survey/.

Gross, L. & McCauley, C. (2020). *Digital Readiness Technical Manual [unpublished manuscript]*. Greensboro, NC: Center for Creative Leadership.

Gurvis, J., McCauley, C., & Swofford, M. (2016). *Putting experience at the center of talent management*. Greensboro, NC: Center for Creative Leadership.

Holtzblatt, K. & Marsden, N. (2018). Retaining women in technology. *2018 IEEE International Conference on Engineering, Technology, and Innovation (ICE/ITMC)* (pp. 1–8). IEEE

Huber, C., Sukharevsky, A., & Zemmel, R. (2021). *How boards can help digital transformations*. McKinsey Digital. https://www.mckinsey.com/business-functions/mckinsey-digital/our-insights/how-boards-can-help-digital-transformations.

Hund, K., La Porta, D., Fabregas, T. P., Laing, T., & Drexhage, J. (2020). *Minerals for climate action: The mineral intensity of the clean energy transition*. The World Bank. https://pubdocs.worldbank.org/en/961711588875536384/Minerals-for-Climate-Action-The-Mineral-Intensity-of-the-Clean-Energy-Transition.pdf.

Hurth, V., Ebert, C., & Prabhu, J. (2018). Purpose: The construct and its antecedents and consequences (No. 2). working paper.

Hutchinson, R., Maher, H., de Laubier, R., & Charanya, T. (2022). *The five digital building blocks of a corporate sustainability agenda*. Boston Consulting

Group. https://www.bcg.com/publications/2022/building-blocks-of-corporate-sustainability-agenda.

Ibarra, H., Carter, M. N., & Silva, C. (2010). Why men still get more promotions than women. *Harvard Business Review*, 88(9), 80–85.

ICCR's 2022 Proxy Resolutions and Voting Guidelines. (2022, February 16). Interfaith Center for Corporate Responsibility. https://www.iccr.org/sites/default/files/iccrs_2022_proxy_resolutions_and_voting_guide_v2.pdf.

Johnson, B. (2011). *Polarity Management: Identifying and Managing Unsolvable Problems*. HRD Press.

Johnson, S. K., Hekman, D. R., & Chan, E. T. (2016). If there's only one woman in your candidate pool, there's statistically no chance she'll be hired. *Harvard Business Review*, 26(4), 1–7.

Kapor Center. (2020). *The black technology workforce: Designing a more inclusive future*. https://www.kaporcenter.org/wp-content/uploads/2021/02/KC21001_black-tech-workforce-report_v4.pdf.

Kegan, R. (1982). *The Evolving Self: Problem and Process in Human Development*. Harvard University Press.

Kegan, R. & Lahey, L. (2009). *Immunity to Change: How to Overcome It and Unlock the Potential in Yourself and Your Organization*. Harvard Business Review Press.

Kolb, D. (1984). *Experiential Learning: Experience As the Source of Learning and Development*. Prentice-Hall.

Korn Ferry. *Future of work: The global talent crunch*. (2018). https://www.kornferry.com/content/dam/kornferry/docs/pdfs/KF-Future-of-Work-Talent-Crunch-Report.pdf.

Koval, C. Z. & Rosette, A. S. (2021). The natural hair bias in job recruitment. *Social Psychological and Personality Science*, 12(5), 741–750.

Leslie, J. (2021). *Pandemic paradoxes and how they affect your workers*. Greensboro, NC: Center for Creative Leadership.

Li, T.-T., Wang, K., Sueyoshi, T., & Wang, D. D. (2021). ESG: Research Progress and Future Prospects. *Sustainability*, 13(21), 11663. MDPI AG.

Lokuge, S., Sedera, D., Grover, V., & Xu, D. (2019). Organizational readiness for digital innovation: Development and empirical calibration of a construct. *Information and Management*, 56, 445–461.

Lorenzo, R., Voight, N., Schetelig, K., Zawadzki, A., Welpe, I., & Brosi, P. (2017). *The Mix that Matters: Innovation through Diversity*. Boston Consulting Group. https://www.bcg.com/publications/2017/people-organization-leadership-talent-innovation-through-diversity-mix-that-matters.

Maennling, N. & Toledano, P. (2019). *Seven trends shaping the future of the mining and metals industry.* World Economic Forum. https://www.weforum.org/agenda/2019/03/seven-trends-shaping-the-future-of-the-mining-and-metals-sector/.

Marsh, H. W., Huppert, F. A., Donald, J. N., Horwood, M. S., & Sahdra, B. K. (2020). The well-being profile (WB-Pro): Creating a theoretically based multidimensional measure of well-being to advance theory, research, policy, and practice. *Psychological Assessment*, (32)3, 294–313.

Matias, C. (2018). Tell the devil I'm back: A self-reflection on the radical possibilities for racial justice. *Taboo: The Journal of Culture and Education*, 17(1), 2.

McGuire, J. & Palus, C. (2019). *Vertical leadership for executive teams: Culture still wins over strategy.* Greensboro, NC: Center for Creative Leadership.

Mezirow, J., & Taylor, E. W. (Eds.). (2009). Transformative learning in practice: Insights from community, workplace, and higher education. John Wiley & Sons.

Mikalsen, M., Moe, N. B., Stray, V., & Nyrud, H. (2018). Agile digital transformation: a case study of interdependencies. In *Proceedings of the 39th International Conference on Information Systems (ICIS)*. Association for Information Systems (AIS).

Mirković, V., Lukic, J., & Lazarevic, S. (2019). Key characteristics of organizational structure. In *24th International Scientific Symposium Strategic Management and Decision Support Systems in Strategic Management*.

Mining and Metallurgical Society of America. (2021). *Recycling — A part of the lifecycle of minerals.* https://www.mmsa.net/pdfs/RecyclingFactSheet101521.pdf.

Nahavandi, S. (2019). Industry 5.0 — A human-centric solution. *Sustainability*, 11(16), 4371.

Nielsen, M. W. (2017). Gender diversity leads to better science. *Proceedings of the National Academy of Sciences*, 114(8), 1740–1742.

Palus, C. J., McGuire, J. B., Stawiski, S., & Torbert, W. R. (2020). The art and science of vertical development. In *Maturing leadership: How adult development impacts leadership*. Emerald Publishing Limited.

Piaget, J. (1941). The mechanism of mental development. *Archives of Psychology*, 28, 218–249.

Rokeach, M. (1960). *The Open and Closed Mind.* Basic Books.

Rooke, D. & Torbert, W. R. (2005). Seven transformations of leadership: leaders are made, not born, and how they develop is critical for organizational change. *Harvard Business Review*, 83(4), 66–76.

Ruderman, M. & Ernst, C. (2010). Finding yourself how social identity affects leadership. *Leadership in Action*, 30(1), 14–18.

Ruderman, M. N., Clerkin, C., & Fernandez, K. C. (2022). *Resilience That Works: Eight Practices for Leadership and Life*. Greensboro, NC: Center for Creative Leadership.

Schein, E. H. & Bennis, W. (1965). *Personal and Organizational Change via Group Methods*. Wiley.

Scholz, R. W., Bartlesman, E. J., Diefenbach, S., Franke, L., Grunwold, A., Helbing, D., …, Pereiza, G. V. (2018). Unintended side effects of the digital transition: European scientists' messages from a proposition-based expert round table. *Sustainability*, 10, 2001.

Schrage, M., Pring, B., Kiron, D., & Dickerson, D. (2021). *Leadership's digital transformation: Leading purposefully in an era of context collapse*. MIT Sloan Management Review. https://sloanreview.mit.edu/projects/leaderships-digital-transformation/.

Schwab, K. (2017). *The Fourth Industrial Revolution*. Crown Business.

Schumpeter, J. (1939). *Business Cycles*. McGraw Hill.

Society for Mining, Metallurgy, & Exploration. (2021, December). *Meeting the world's future mineral needs*. https://www.smenet.org/What-We-Do/Technical-Briefings/Meeting-the-World-s-Future-Mineral-Needs.

Stansberry, K., Anderson, J., & Rainie, L. (2019). *Experts Optimistic about the Next 50 years of Digital Life*. Pew Research Center.

Torbert, W. (1972). *Learning from Experience: Toward Consciousness*. Columbia University Press.

United Nations. (2007). United National Declaration of the Rights of Indigenous Peoples. https://www.un.org/development/desa/indigenouspeoples/wp-content/uploads/sites/19/2018/11/UNDRIP_E_web.pdf.

US Department of Labor. (2019). *Percentage of women workers in science, technology, engineering and math (STEM)*. https://www.dol.gov/agencies/wb/data/occupations-stem.

van Tuin, L., Schaufeli, W., Van den Broeck, A., & van Rhenen, W. (2020). A corporate purpose as an antecedent to employee motivation and work engagement. *Frontiers in Psychology*, 11, 572343.

Warner, K. & Wager, M. (2019). Building dynamic capabilities for digital transformation: An ongoing process of strategic renewal. *Long Range Planning*, 52, 326–349.

Wasch, S. (2021, September 22). *Missed opportunities in providing pandemic relief funds*. Field Center for Children's Policy, Practice and Research. https://fieldcenteratpenn.org/missed-opportunities-in-providing-pandemic-relief-funds/.

Weill, P., Apel, T., Woerner, S. L., & Banner, S. J. (2019). It pays to have a digitally savvy board. *MIT Sloan Management Review*, 60(3), 41–45.

Weise, K. & Metz, C. (2023, February 16). Microsoft considers more limits for its new A.I. chatbot. *New York Times*.

Well-Being Concepts. (2018). Centers for Disease Control and Prevention. https://www.cdc.gov/hrqol/wellbeing.htm.

West, S. M. (2020). Redistribution and rekognition: A feminist critique of algorithmic fairness. *Catalyst: Feminism, Theory, Technoscience*, 6(2), 1–24.

Windt, B., Borgman, H., & Amrit, C. (2019). Understanding leadership challenges and responses in data-driven transformations. *Proceedings of the 52nd Hawaii International Conference on System Sciences* (pp. 4987–4996).

World Health Organization. (2019). Burn-out an "occupational phenomenon": International classification of diseases. https://www.who.int/news/item/28-05-2019-burn-out-an-occupational-phenomenon-international-classification-of-diseases.

Wormington, S. & Loignon, A. (2022). *Psychologically safe for some, but not all? The downsides of assuming shared psychological safety among senior leadership teams*. Greensboro, NC: Center for Creative Leadership.

Wu, J., Wang, N., Mei, W., & Liu, L. (2020). Technology-induced job anxiety during non-work time: Examining conditional effects of techno-invasion on job anxiety. *International Journal of Networking and Virtual Organisations*, 22(2), 162–182.

Young, S. F., Leslie, J. B., Balakrishnan, R., & Winn, B. (2021). The chief of leadership development: Preparing today's leaders for tomorrow's challenges. *People & Strategy*, 44(2), 52–56.

Zahidi, S. (2020, January). We need a global reskilling revolution–here's why. In *World Economic Forum* (Vol. 22, pp. 117–118).

Index

www.ingramcontent.com/pod-product-compliance
Lightning Source LLC
Chambersburg PA
CBHW050601190326
41458CB00007B/2130